THE LIQUID STATE

Physical Sciences

Editor

PROFESSOR G. O. JONES

Professor of Physics in the University of London

THE LIQUID STATE

J. A. Pryde
B.SC., PH.D.

Senior Lecturer in Physics
Sir John Cass College, London

HUTCHINSON UNIVERSITY LIBRARY

LONDON

HUTCHINSON & CO (*Publishers*) LTD
178–202 Great Portland Street, London W.1

London Melbourne Sydney
Auckland Bombay Toronto
Johannesburg New York

★

First published 1966

*The cover design of the paperback edition is by
courtesy of B. J. Alder and T. E. Wainwright.
It illustrates 'molecular' motion in fluid (see p. 118)*

*This book has been set in Times New Roman type face.
It has been printed in Great Britain by William Clowes
and Sons Ltd, London and Beccles, on Smooth Wove
paper and bound by Wm Brendon of Tiptree, Essex*

CONTENTS

ACKNOWLEDGMENTS

I should like to thank the following for permission to make use of copyright material: John Wiley & Son Ltd. for fig. 2.2; Dr N. S. Gingrich and the American Institute of Physics for figs. 3.1 and 3.2; Taylor & Frances Ltd. for fig. 3.3; The Faraday Society for table 4.1; The Royal Society for fig. 6.2; Pergamon Press Ltd. for table 6.1; W. W. Wood, J. D. Jacobson, T. W. Wainwright and the American Institute of Physics for fig. 7.2; Professor A. A. Broyles and the American Institute of Physics for fig. 8.1; Professor G. D. Scott and *Nature* for fig. 8.3.

PREFACE

This book is an attempt to provide for undergraduate and post-graduate students a simplified treatment of some recent molecular theories of the liquid state of matter. Whereas existing text-books on the properties of matter give much attention to the kinetic–molecular theory of gases and solids, a corresponding treatment of liquids is very generally neglected. The reasons for this neglect are readily understandable; those theories of liquids which can reasonably make some claim to be based on fundamental physical principles are of relatively modern creation, some of the theoretical background is unfamiliar to students, and, finally, the theories themselves inevitably involve some rather complex mathematics.

In seeking to minimise these difficulties I have thought it advisable to confine the treatment to those simple monatomic fluids whose properties can be adequately discussed in terms of classical physics, omitting the treatment of quantum fluids. The first eight chapters cover the equilibrium properties, and include a brief exposition of the necessary thermodynamic and statistical mechanical foundation. The extra complications which arise in non-equilibrium situations form the subject of the last two chapters and are illustrated by their application to the specific property of liquid shear viscosity.

In the mathematical presentation I have tried to steer a middle course, bearing in mind the likely mathematical limitations of the intended reader. On the one hand, to attempt to discuss theories of liquids without frequent references to fundamental principles would leave the reader with no yardstick with which to judge the status and worth of the theories. On the other hand, liquid theory is peculiarly prone to the danger remarked on by S. G. Brush in a recent review article; that of subjecting the unfortunate reader to hundreds of complex mathematical equations without rewarding him with any real solution to the problem. To avoid this discouraging situation I have tried to relate the necessary mathematics to the physical ideas they express, omitting lengthy justifications of particular steps when these would seem to add little to the physical development. Those readers who wish to pursue the subject more deeply will find suggestions for further reading at the end of the book.

My best thanks are due to Professor G. O. Jones and Dr A. Suddaby for many helpful criticisms. I should also like to thank Mrs M. Skinner and Mrs B. Champion for their help in typing the manuscript.

JOHN PRYDE

I

SOLIDS, LIQUIDS AND GASES

To the philosophers of antiquity the complex nature of the material world could be interpreted by a Theory of Elements, that is, a theory which attempts to reduce the diverse properties of materials to a small number of simpler properties. In different cultures and at different times ideas about the number and nature of these Elements varied. To Aristotle (384–322 B.C.), whose thinking influenced European ideas for two thousand years, the number of these Elements was four: Earth, Air, Fire and Water. Each Element could be distinguished by its qualities; Earth embodied the qualities of coldness and dryness, Air was hot and fluid, Fire hot and dry, and Water cold and fluid. Every substance was compounded of the four Elements: the differences between substances depended on the proportions in which they were present. Thus a piece of green wood when heated exudes water, therefore wood contains the element Water; steam and pungent vapours are given off, therefore wood contains Air; the wood burns, therefore it contains Fire; and an ash is left, therefore it contains Earth. Highly combustible substances contain much Fire, all liquids much Water and so on.

It is difficult for us today, with our minds conditioned by twentieth-century concepts about matter, to grasp precisely how the ancients understood these ideas. Certainly we must not imagine that the names given to the Elements are used in their modern sense. We still, however, divide matter into three states, solid, liquid and gas, and this division preserves something of the old ideas of Earth, Water and Air. We see other traces of their survival in the modern chemist's use of the terms 'alkaline earths', 'rare earths' (to the medieval alchemist an earth was a non-metallic solid unchanged by fire), while water in the Latin *aqua* survives in *aqua regia, aqua fortis*. The word 'gas' was coined by Van Helmont (1577–1644) and is derived from the same root as 'chaos', implying a wild movement of particles; it eventually replaced the term 'air' as in 'inflammable air' (hydrogen) and 'fixed air' (carbon dioxide). The fourth Element, Fire, appears in modern dress as 'heat energy', a concept arrived at historically via the notions of phlogiston and caloric.

Our modern way of explaining the behaviour of matter has developed from another ancient idea, the Atomic Theory, which in part supplemented and in part conflicted with the theory of the Elements. The origin of the idea that matter is composed of 'solid massy hard impenetrable moveable particles...incomparably harder than any porous bodies compounded of them; even so very hard as never to wear or break in pieces', as Newton expressed it,[1] is usually attributed to the Greek philosopher Democritus, but the concept remained largely a sterile speculation until Dalton and others revived it to build the foundation of modern chemistry. In the eighteenth and nineteenth centuries the atomic theory made much progress in spite of the fact that atoms and molecules were often regarded as convenient mathematical fictions, useful in theory, but having no real existence.

Outside chemistry the atomic theory had its most striking success in accounting for the properties of gases. These were visualised as composed of myriads of molecules in rapid, random and unceasing motion and it was assumed that Newton's laws of motion could be applied to the molecules just as they could to the motion of billiard balls or cannon balls. From this Kinetic Theory of Gases came the first estimates of the number, size and speed of molecules in a given quantity of gas. The properties of the molecules were thus inferred from the bulk properties of matter, and from those of gases in particular.

As time went on and the reality of molecules began to be generally accepted, the emphasis changed. More and more was discovered about the structure and properties of atoms and molecules. From the properties of individual molecules and knowledge of the forces which molecules exert on each other, it should be possible, it was thought, to calculate how matter in bulk behaves when compressed, or heated, or otherwise experimented upon. Modern theories of the properties of matter are essentially attempts to do this. The difficulty is to find some way of calculating mathematically the effect of the interactions between the enormous number of molecules in any quantity of matter which is big enough to make experiments on.

Of the three states of matter gases are the easiest to handle mathematically because the molecules are, on average, so far apart that the forces they exert on each other can, to begin with, be disregarded or regarded as only existing during brief 'collisions'. Thus the kinetic theory of gases was brought to an advanced state of development by the end of the nineteenth century. In solids and liquids the molecules are so close together that any molecule is always subject to large forces by its neighbours. The atoms in a solid are, however, arranged in a regular geometrical pattern and this greatly simplifies the calculation of the properties. When this regular arrangement was fully grasped at the beginning of the twentieth century the theory of the solid state made rapid progress.

Progress towards the understanding of the behaviour of liquids has been much slower. The molecules in liquids are closely spaced but are in no extended regular order and this has made study of the interactions difficult. Only in the last thirty years or so have real advances been made. In part these advances have been due to regarding liquids as intermediate in their properties between solids and gases, and it will be helpful to begin our study of the liquid state by surveying the three states of matter, to see in what ways they resemble each other and in what ways they differ.

The most obvious differences between solids on the one hand and liquids and gases on the other, is that a solid maintains its shape indefinitely if left undisturbed. Liquids and gases must be kept in a container. The container for a liquid need not have a lid, the liquid will take up the shape of the container to the level of the free surface. It is this free surface which distinguishes a liquid from a gas. A gas, as it were, cannot provide itself with a boundary surface but will always take up the entire volume available to it. It must be kept in a completely closed container.

The ability of a solid to keep its shape is expressed by saying that it can support indefinitely a shear stress (provided that this stress is not too great). Fluids—the word includes liquids and gases—cannot support shear stresses no matter how small, but yield and flow in response to them.

Liquids and solids, on the other hand, resemble each other in having the property of cohesion. The molecules do not fly apart from each other as in a gas and so liquids and solids can maintain a boundary surface. The close packing of the molecules in solids and liquids is shown by their densities. The densities of common liquids and solids do not differ greatly and the change in density when a solid melts is on average only about 10%. The densities of gases are about one hundred to one thousand times smaller than liquids or solids.

The close packing of molecules in solids and liquids is again demonstrated in the way in which these states resist compression. In order to decrease the volume of a solid or liquid by even a small amount very large pressures must be applied. For example, to decrease the volume of water by 1% at ordinary temperatures a pressure of 220 atm must be applied. To similarly reduce the volume of a gas initially at atmospheric pressure requires only 0·01 atm.

The intermediate status of liquids appears most clearly when we consider the transformation from one state to the other. At sufficiently low temperatures and high pressures all substances exist as solids; at sufficiently high temperatures and low pressures as gases (provided chemical decomposition does not occur). At intermediate temperatures and pressures the liquid state is the stable one.

Such are the immediately obvious properties of the three states of matter. When we come to examine them a little more critically, however, modification of our ideas must be made. Some substances such as pitch or glass seem to be neither liquid nor solid. A lump of pitch will break or shatter under a blow like any solid, but if left for a long time on a flat surface will deform and flow under its own weight like a liquid. By reducing the temperature the rate of flow can be made so small as to be imperceptible over a long period. This is the case with glass at room temperature, for glass objects from the most ancient tombs retain the shape that they were first given. At higher temperatures glass will begin to soften and flow like a liquid. The interesting thing is that there does not seem to be any sharply defined temperature below which glass can be said to be a solid and above which it is a liquid. This contrasts with the sharp melting temperatures of simple solids such as ice.

The statement that a container for a liquid does not need a lid to prevent the contents from escaping, in contrast to the container for a gas, also needs closer examination. Volatile liquids such as ether or petrol will evaporate from an open container. Indeed, all liquids are volatile, though some, like mercury or heavy oils, evaporate so slowly that their escape goes unnoticed. The same considerations apply to solids. Solids like naphthalene or camphor if left exposed will slowly disappear by the process called sublimation. Every solid or liquid with a perceptible smell shows that molecules must be continually escaping from the boundary surface. It is true that the rate of escape of the molecules from most solids is immeasurably small but this does not alter the principle. In scientific language the situation is described by saying that under ordinary conditions solids or liquids in open containers are not in thermodynamic equilibrium. Now it is much easier to study matter which is in equilibrium and this we can easily arrange if we suppose that matter, whether solid, liquid or gas, is always to be imagined kept in a closed container. If this container takes the form of a hollow cylinder with a close-fitting piston which can move freely back and forth then we may study the effect of varying the volume available to the substance inside. To avoid complications we may imagine that all the air has been pumped out of the cylinder before the substance is introduced, so that inside we have only a pure substance in the form of a solid, liquid or gas, or combinations of these states co-existing in equilibrium. We may disturb the equilibrium by moving the piston or by changing the temperature. When we do this, evaporation or sublimation or condensation may occur until a new equilibrium is attained.

This isolation of our substance from the outside world has a further advantage. Some of the immediately obvious distinctions between the three states of matter are, in a sense, accidental. They occur because we live on a planet where the temperature and barometric pressure do not vary very much from day to day. If we lived on a planet where the atmospheric pressure was one hundred times greater than on our own the densities of gases would approach those of solids and liquids. Again, in everyday life, we tend to attribute too great a significance to the boiling point as marking the change from liquid to vapour; but the boiling point is of no universal significance because it can be changed at will by changing the pressure. When isolated from the effect of atmospheric pressure by our closed container the boiling temperature loses its significance as a marker on the temperature scale separating the liquid and gaseous forms of a substance. What is to take its place?

The conditions under which the liquid and gaseous states of the same substance can exist side by side in equilibrium were investigated by Caignard de la Tour in 1822 and by Andrews in 1869. From these researches emerged the concept of the critical temperature. Below the critical temperature it is possible for a substance to co-exist in the liquid and vapour forms separated by a boundary surface. Above the critical temperature it is impossible to distinguish a boundary separating two regions having different physical properties.

How this state of affairs comes about may be seen by following in imagination an experiment with our closed container. Let us imagine that it is about one-third full of a liquid—say water—at room temperature, 20°C. The space above the liquid is filled only with water vapour. This vapour exerts a pressure, the saturated vapour pressure for water, which is about 0·023 atm at 20°C. There is no difficulty in distinguishing the liquid and vapour states, presuming we can see inside. The boundary surface is distinct and the liquid is dense while the vapour is tenuous. Their densities are 0·998 and $1·85 \times 10^{-5}$ gm cm^{-3} respectively.

Let us now heat the container, keeping the piston fixed in position in all that follows. The higher temperature causes some of the liquid to evaporate, the molecules passing into the vapour space, so that the vapour becomes more dense and the pressure inside increases. At the same time the increase in temperature causes the liquid to expand slightly so that it becomes less dense. As the temperature continues to rise it will pass 100°C, the normal boiling point of water, but this will not be marked by the onset of boiling as it would if water were heated in an open vessel. The pressure in the container will reach 1 atm as the temperature reaches 100°C but as there is no communication with the outside there will be nothing to distinguish this particular temperature from any other. At 350°C we shall still be able to distinguish a boundary marking off the liquid and vapour regions. The pressure inside is now 163 atm and as a consequence the density of the vapour is high, about 0·114 gm cm^{-3}. On the other hand the thermal expansion of the liquid has been going on continuously, in spite of the increasing pressure on it, so that its density has now fallen to 0·575 gm cm^{-3}. If we continue to heat the vessel the density of the vapour continues to increase and that of the liquid to decrease until eventually they become equal. For water this happens at a temperature of 374·15°C, the pressure being 218·3 atm and the density 0·32 gm cm^{-3}, these being the critical temperature, critical pressure and critical density respectively. If we continue to heat the container we find that, instead of a liquid and gaseous state, we have a uniform density of matter in the container with no boundary surface.

Not only do the densities of the two states become identical at the critical temperature but all other physical properties which serve to distinguish between the liquid and the gas become identical at, or at any rate very close to, the critical temperature. The surface tension of the liquid, the latent heat of vaporisation, the difference in the refractive indices of liquid and vapour (by which we were able to observe the boundary), all vanish above the critical temperature. Nor can the vanished boundary between liquid and vapour be restored by moving the piston in or out. The density may be varied from a very low value which we should normally think characteristic of a gas up to a high value characteristic of ordinary liquids, but no separation into liquid and gaseous parts is observed. The substance is neither liquid nor gaseous but simply fluid. The critical temperature, and not the boiling point, is the natural upper temperature limit to the liquid state.

The low-temperature limit of existence of the liquid state is ordinarily thought of as the freezing point, that is, the temperature at which a solid begins to form when a liquid is cooled at atmospheric pressure.

Again, this temperature can be changed by changing the pressure, though it is true that the change in freezing (or melting) temperature with pressure is much less than the change in boiling temperature. Nevertheless, if we wish to be precise, we must eliminate the effects of atmospheric pressure by returning again to our piston and cylinder. If we cool the system we shall find that ice begins to form at a temperature very close to, but not exactly equal to, the freezing point. This temperature is the Triple Point Temperature and for water is nearly 0·01°C greater than the melting temperature. The reason for the name is that, if the temperature is maintained exactly at the triple point, the three states solid, liquid and vapour can co-exist in equilibrium. If we reduce the temperature below the triple point all the liquid will freeze, leaving only ice and water vapour. The triple point therefore marks the natural low-temperature limit of existence of the liquid state.

The equilibrium between the three states can be represented on a diagram in which the pressure, p, in the cylinder is plotted against the absolute temperature, T. For simple substances the diagram has the form of fig. 1.1.

The curve T_r–C shows the way these quantities vary when the cylinder contains only liquid and vapour. It therefore terminates at the critical point C and the triple point T_r, for outside these limits no liquid–vapour combination is possible. Below the triple point the curve O–T_r represents the vapour pressure of the states solid and vapour. It goes to the absolute zero of temperature, at which all the vapour would condense, leaving a perfect vacuum and so zero pressure on the piston. It is called the sublimation curve.

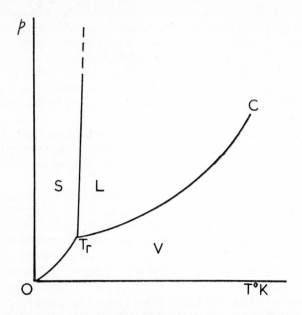

Fig. 1.1   The phase diagram of a simple substance. A continuous transition from vapour to liquid is possible, i.e. without crossing the curve T_r–C. No such continuous path has been found for the transition solid–liquid or solid-vapour

The third, nearly vertical, curve starting at the triple point represents the equilibrium between the remaining possible combination of the three states, that is, one in which only liquid and solid are present but no vapour. To obtain this combination we must condense all the vapour by pushing in the piston until its face rests on the surface of the liquid. Then, by applying large pressures and by adjusting the temperature we may investigate how the melting point changes with pressure. This gives the melting curve. It is always very steep, showing that to change the melting point even slightly very large pressures must be applied.

For most substances the melting point is raised by increasing the pressure, but for water it is lowered by one degree for a pressure increase of 135 atm.

No upper termination to the melting curve is shown on the diagram and none has ever been found experimentally. If such a point exists it would be analogous to the critical point on the saturated vapour curve, and it would be possible, by suitable adjustments of pressure and temperature, to pass continuously from the solid to the liquid state without observing a discontinuity in any physical property. The melting curve has been followed[2] for helium up to 7270 atm and 50°K, and for argon up to 8250 atm and 234°K, with no indication of a termination. These figures may be compared with the respective critical data which are 2 atm and 5°K for helium, and 48 atm and 151°K for argon. Moreover, there was no indication in the experiments that the densities or other properties of the solid and liquid were approaching a common value as the pressure increased. The Law of Corresponding States (ch. 2) suggests that, if substances like helium and argon with low critical pressures and temperatures do not show an upper limit with presently attainable pressures, other substances with higher critical constants are unlikely to show one either.

The p–V diagram of a simple fluid

Instead of varying the temperature while keeping the volume constant we may instead vary the volume while keeping the temperature constant. The results of such experiments are conveniently represented on a diagram in which the pressure, p, is plotted against the volume, V (fig. 1.2).

Let us imagine that we start with our piston and cylinder containing water at about room temperature, 20°C. Suppose that the piston has been pulled out so far that all the liquid has evaporated so that the cylinder contains only vapour at a low pressure. This may be represented by the point A in the diagram. If the piston is now pushed in, keeping the temperature constant, the volume will decrease and the pressure will rise in a manner roughly described by Boyle's Law, $pV=$ const., until the point B is reached. At this point the pressure is 0·023 atm. If we continue to push in the piston, drops of liquid appear in the inner surfaces of the cylinder and, as the piston moves in, the volume of liquid increases. The pressure, however, remains steady;

attempts to increase it by pushing in the piston further merely cause
more vapour to condense. In this way we trace out the horizontal
line BC.

At C the condensation of the vapour is complete. The face of the
piston rests on the surface of the liquid and there is no space between
them for the vapour. If we continue to push on the piston we encounter a greatly increased resistance due to the relatively incompressible
liquid. To produce a very small decrease in volume large pressures

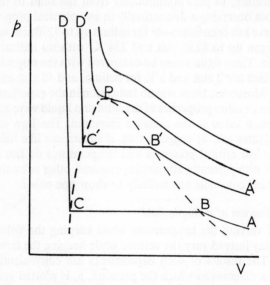

Fig. 1.2   The isothermals of a simple fluid

must be applied, so that the curve shoots almost vertically upward
along CD.

Suppose now the whole experiment is repeated at a higher temperature, say 100°C, giving the curve A'B'C'D'. The general shape
of this curve is the same as ABCD but with the following differences.
First, the pressure at any volume is higher throughout because of the
higher temperature. Condensation of the first drop of liquid at B'
does not occur until a pressure of 1 atm and the volume at B' is much
less than the volume at B. The volume at C', on the other hand, is

slightly greater than at C because at the higher temperature the liquid has expanded. Thus the flat part B′C′ is shorter than BC.

If we repeat the experiment at higher and higher temperatures we find the flat part, the liquid–vapour region, becomes shorter and shorter until for a particular isothermal its length is reduced to zero at the point P. This is the critical point and the isothermal on which it lies is the critical isothermal. If we perform our experiment at any temperature above the critical we produce merely a continuous increase in pressure with decrease in volume, but no condensation takes place.

It should be said that figs 1.1 and 1.2 are not drawn to scale, the ranges of pressures and volumes occurring in our experiments being too great to accommodate on the diagrams. Nevertheless, the general shape of the curves enables us to visualise very easily the behaviour of a fluid. In fig. 1.2 the dotted curve PB′B etc. is the saturated vapour curve; it marks the onset of condensation. The region to the right of it below the critical isothermal is that of the unsaturated vapour. Similarly the curve PC′C etc. is the saturated liquid line, to the left of it the substance is entirely liquid. Between these is the mixture region. Above the critical isothermal no division of the diagram into these regions can be made. In the mixture region the curves are strictly horizontal, showing that the saturated vapour pressure depends only on the temperature and not on the proportions of liquid and vapour present.

This fact provides a rather delicate experimental test for the purity of the liquid. If the flat part is not strictly horizontal it is an indication that the liquid is impure, or that all the air was not pumped out of the system before the experiments were begun.

The critical constants of a number of fluids are given in table 2.1 of ch. 2. Those gases whose critical temperatures lie below room temperature, such as nitrogen and oxygen, cannot be liquified by pressure alone without strong cooling. Early attempts to liquify them failed, and these substances were therefore called the permanent gases. Andrews' work explained why these experiments failed and showed the necessity of cooling below the critical temperature if liquefaction was to be achieved.

2

LIQUIDS CONSIDERED AS DENSE GASES

The fact that in the critical region one may increase the density of a fluid continuously from a very low value characteristic of a gas up to a value approximating to that of ordinary liquids, suggests that one possible approach to the study of the liquid state is to investigate how the molecular interactions in gases change as the gas is compressed.

In an ideal monatomic gas the molecules may be regarded as mass points in random motion with varying speeds but exerting no forces on each other. The kinetic theory of ideal gases begins with this concept. The pressure of the gas is due to the bombardment of the walls of the container by these molecules, the energy of the gas, U, is the sum of the kinetic energies of the molecules. The theory leads to a relation between the pressure, temperature and volume of a given mass of gas, the Equation of State. For one gram molecule this may be written

$$pV = RT \qquad 2.1$$

The total energy of the gas molecules is entirely kinetic energy and is given by

$$U = \tfrac{3}{2} RT \qquad 2.2$$

which is called the Caloric Equation of State. R is the universal gas constant, 8·317 joules deg^{-1} mole^{-1} or 1·98 cal deg^{-1} mole^{-1}. These equations refer to a fixed number of molecules N, Avogadro's number, equal to $6 \cdot 06 \times 10^{23}$. If the temperature is kept constant, 2.1 leads to Boyle's Law, the pressure varies inversely as the volume. Thus the

$p-V$ diagram for an ideal gas consists of a series of rectangular hyperbolae, asymptotic to the p and V axes.

Real gases, or vapours, approximate to ideal gases only if the density is low, that is, the volume is so great that the molecules are, on average, a long way apart from each other. As the gas is compressed this average distance decreases and the effects of the intermolecular forces become apparent. The ideal gas equation of state must then be replaced by an equation which attempts to allow for these forces.

The force between two molecules may be either attractive or repulsive, depending on the distance between the centres of the molecules. If this distance is large the force is attractive but changes to a strong repulsion at short distances. The attraction accounts for the condensation of gases and the cohesion of liquids and solids, the repulsion explains the strong resistance of the condensed states to further compression. This large increase in resistance to compression in liquids and solids suggests that the repulsive force increases very rapidly indeed as the distance between the molecules is decreased below a fairly sharply defined limit.

A more realistic picture of a simple molecule would, then, result if we visualise it not as a point mass but as a hard sphere surrounded by an attractive field of force. If we adopt this model we find that for simple molecules the effective diameter of the sphere comes out in the range of 2·5 to 6 Ångstrom units (1 A.U. $= 10^{-8}$ cm).

The field of force round the sphere extends, theoretically, to infinity, but practically speaking its effects extend to only several times the diameter of the sphere. If the average distances between molecules is more than, say, ten molecular diameters the fluid will show only slight deviations from ideal gas behaviour.

Van der Waals' equation of state

The earliest and most famous attempt to allow for the intermolecular forces is that of J. D. van der Waals (1873), who modified the volume and pressure terms in the ideal gas equation to allow for the repulsive and attractive forces respectively. First, because of the finite volume of the molecules, he supposed that the volume of the container, V, must be replaced by a volume $(V-b)$ where b is a constant which, for hard spheres is, as we shall show later, four times the total volume of the N molecules. To allow for the attractions we note that their effect is to tend to bring the molecules closer together in the same way as the external pressure. These forces may then be represented by an extra pressure, the internal pressure p_1, added to the applied pressure p. The ideal gas law then becomes

$$(p+p_1)(V-b) = RT \qquad 2.3$$

Van der Waals suggested that p_1 varied as the square of the density or, for a fixed mass of gas, as the inverse square of the volume, so that van der Waals' equation of state is

$$\left(p+\frac{a}{V^2}\right)(V-b) = RT \qquad 2.4$$

where a is a constant which is a measure of the strength of the attractive force between a pair of molecules.

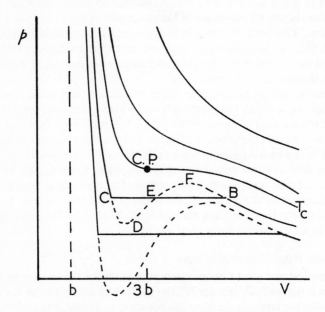

Fig. 2.1   Van der Waals' equation of state

To test this equation one fixes the value of T and plots the variation of pressure with volume. By repeating with different values of T a series of isothermal curves is obtained, as shown in fig. 2.1. These isothermals approach the vertical line $V=b$, for p becomes infinite as V approaches b from larger values.

For high temperatures p decreases continuously as V increases and at large volumes the isothermals approximate to the hyperbolae of the ideal gas law. At lower temperatures sinuous curves are obtained, over parts of which the pressure increases as the volume increases. This clearly represents an unstable state of affairs. The usual interpretation is that the region of the sinuous curves corresponds to the separation of the fluid into liquid and vapour, and that the equation here breaks down. A theoretical isothermal CDEFB must then be replaced by a horizontal line CB. An argument due to Maxwell suggests that this line should be drawn so as to make the areas CDEC and EFBE equal. With this rather enforced modification a general resemblance of fig. 2.1 to the actual isothermals of a real fluid is obtained (fig. 1.2).

At the higher temperature the maxima and minima of the sinuous curves approach each other so that the length of the real horizontal isotherm decreases and finally vanishes at a particular temperature, T_c, which may therefore be identified with the critical temperature.

This permits a deduction of the values of the constants a and b for a fluid. At the critical point the critical isothermal has a horizontal tangent $(\partial p/\partial V)_T = 0$ and also a point of inflexion $(\partial^2 p/\partial V^2)_T = 0$. On calculating these derivatives one has, with the original equation, three equations to determine the critical pressure, volume and temperature in terms of a, b and R, the results being

$$V_c = 3b \qquad T_c = \frac{8a}{27Rb} \qquad p_c = \frac{a}{27b^2} \qquad\qquad 2.5$$

from any two of which the constants a and b may be found. It is usual to determine a and b from the last two, as the critical pressure and temperature are most easily and accurately measurable. With the values of b so obtained one may then calculate the values expected for the critical volume (equal to $3b$) and compare them with the experimental values. The table shows that the calculated values are too high. Furthermore the dimensionless quantity $(RT_c)/(p_c V_c)$ has, for the equation, the value $\frac{8}{3} = 2 \cdot 67$ while the experimental values are distinctly greater than this. For fluids with non-polar molecules of quasi-spherical shape $RT_c/p_c V_c$ has a value close to 3·45. The critical volumes in the table are in litres per mole. The critical density, ρ_c, in gm cm^{-3} is therefore given by $\rho_c = M/1000V_c$ where M is the molecular weight. The measured critical densities for most fluids lie in the range 0·2 to 0·6 gm cm^{-3}. One might expect that with such close packing of molecules any equation based on simple arguments about molecular forces would fail.

The sinuous parts of the isothermals, CDEFB represent, as has been said, unstable states. This unstable region may, however, be divided into three parts. Between D and F the slope is positive and this represents a mechanically impossible situation. Between C and D and F and B the slope is negative so that mechanical stability is possible. Under special conditions parts of these curves can be realised. If, for example, one compresses an unsaturated vapour, liquid droplets normally form at the saturation point B, but if the space is

TABLE 2.1

Critical data and van der Waals' constants

$(R = 0.08206 \text{ l atm mole}^{-1} \text{ deg}^{-1} \text{ K})$

Fluid	a $\text{l}^2 \text{ atm}$ mole^{-2}	b l mole^{-1}	p_c atm	T_c °K	V_c l mole^{-1}	$3b$ l mole^{-1}	$RT_c/p_c V_c$
He(4)	0·0341	0·0237	2·26	5·3	0·0578	0·0712	3·33
Ne	0·21	0·0171	25·9	44·5	0·0417	0·0513	3·48
A	1·345	0·0322	48·0	150·7	0·0752	0·0966	3·43
Kr	2·32	0·0398	54·3	209·4	0·092	0·119	3·44
Xe	4·19	0·0511	58·0	289·8	0·118	0·153	3·45
H_2	0·244	0·0267	12·8	33·3	0·065	0·080	3·28
N_2	1·39	0·0391	33·5	126·1	0·090	0·117	3·43
O_2	1·36	0·0318	49·7	154·4	0·0745	0·0954	3·43
CH_4	2·25	0·0428	45·8	190·7	0·099	0·128	3·45
CO_2	3·59	0·0427	72·8	304·2	0·094	0·127	3·49
H_2O	5·46	0·0305	218·3	647·4	0·056	0·091	4·34

free from all dust or other nuclei it is possible to produce a *super-saturated* vapour and so follow the curve a little way towards F. Such super-saturated vapours normally have only a fleeting existence since the appearance of a nucleus, or the presence of the walls of the vessel, will serve as growing points for liquid drops and the system then breaks up into the usual liquid–vapour mixture. The Wilson Cloud Chamber employs the phenomenon of super-saturation, dust-free water or alcohol vapour (mixed with air) being brought into the super-saturated state by the cooling produced by sudden expansion. The condensation nuclei are ionising particles, such as those from radioactive elements, and the trail of liquid droplets show the path taken by the particle.

Similarly, a part of CD of the isothermal can be realised by decreasing the pressure on a liquid to below the point C. Normally the liquid would then break up into vapour and liquid and follow CE, that is, it would boil. In a dust-free liquid contained in a vessel with smooth walls boiling is sometimes delayed for a fraction of a second because there are no nuclei on which vapour bubbles can form. The liquid is said to be *superheated*. The phenomenon of 'boiling with bumping', familiar to anyone who has heated a liquid in a smooth-walled vessel, illustrates this superheating. It has again been turned to account in the study of energetic nuclear particles in the Glaser Bubble Chamber. In this device liquid hydrogen is prevented from boiling by an externally applied pressure. If this pressure is suddenly released and the liquid immediately photographed, the trail of an ionising particle is revealed as a line of vapour bubbles where boiling is being initiated. The parts FB and CD, therefore, do represent physically realisable states (meta-stable states), though the stability is precarious.

Further inspection of fig. 2.1 shows that at low temperatures the isothermals intersect the axis of volume, indicating states of negative external pressure. This at first sight seems absurd, yet it has been known for many years that liquids can withstand tensile forces of considerable magnitude. Thus if the space above the mercury in a simple barometer tube, held at an angle to the vertical, is completely filled with a pure liquid, it is possible, on raising the tube to the vertical, to cause the mercury to stand at a height greater than the barometric pressure. The liquid must therefore be under tension, which tension it can support indefinitely. If the liquid be disturbed or agitated it breaks up into a vapour–liquid mixture and the mercury level drops. Meyer in 1911 was able to show that mercury itself can withstand negative pressures of some one hundred atmospheres.

A simple way of demonstrating negative pressures in liquids is to take a short length of clean glass tube sealed at one end and drawn down to a short capillary at the other. This is filled with air and dust-free alcohol or water by heating and cooling until the only vapour space is in the capillary tube. The tube may then be sealed by momentarily inserting the tip in a flame, to give a tube with a small vapour bubble, rather like a spirit-level tube. The tube is now warmed in a water bath until the expansion of the liquid causes the bubble to disappear. The tube is removed and allowed to cool but the bubble of vapour does not reappear at the expected temperature. The liquid is 'stretched' so as to occupy the entire volume. On further cooling the liquid suddenly ruptures with a sharp click and myriads of tiny vapour bubbles form, which rise to the top to re-form the original bubble. Thus the conditions for realising negative pressures in liquids are that the liquid should completely fill the container and that no nuclei should be present.

According to van der Waals' equation negative pressures can exist, provided that the negative external pressure, p, is less than the internal pressure $p_1 = a/V^2$ for then the volume and temperature can still be positive. Setting $p = 0$ and investigating the condition that the resulting quadratic equation in V should have real roots, leads to the conclusion that the temperature should be less than $\frac{27}{32}T_c$. This conclusion is, however, of little real physical significance.

Other equations of state

Since van der Waals put forward his equation many other equations of state have been proposed, in attempts to improve general agreement with experiment or for special purposes. The best-known of these are[1]

Berthelot	$(p + a/TV^2)(V - b) = RT$	2.6
Dieterici	$p(V - b) = RT \exp(-a/RTV)$	2.7
Clausius	$\{p + a/(v + c)^2\}(V - b) = RT$	2.8

Berthelot's and Dieterici's equations contain three constants a, b and R. Clausius' equation has an additional constant c.

All these equations reduce to the ideal gas law as the density approaches zero. All exhibit sinuous isothermals below a certain temperature. For the three-constant equations the constants can be related to the critical data by the procedure used above, the results being summarised in the table below.

Each equation has its advantages and disadvantages. The Dieterici equation gives a value for $RT_c/p_c V_c$ of 3·69, in reasonable agreement with a mean value near 3·45 for the non-polar gases in table 2.1, and is remarkably accurate in the neighbourhood of the critical point. No equation, however, represents the p–V–T data for gases over wide ranges and none is based on a rigorous mathematical treatment of intermolecular forces. The phenomenon of condensation is not predicted by the equations and must be introduced by the same artificial procedure as used above for van der Waals' equation.

The usefulness of such equations of state lies more in the suggestive physical ideas that can be deduced from them rather than in their numerical predictions of experimental data. They provide rough qualitative information about the magnitude of the repulsive and attractive forces (related to the constants b and a respectively). More elaborate equations, some containing up to twenty-five adjustable constants, have been proposed to fit the p–V–T data over wider ranges.

TABLE 2.2

	van der Waals	*Dieterici*	*Berthelot*
p_c	$a/27b^2$	$a/4e^2b^2$	$(aR/216b^3)^{1/2}$
V_c	$3b$	$2b$	$3b$
T_c	$8a/27Rb$	$a/4Rb$	$(a/27Rb)^{1/2}$
RT_c/p_cV_c	$8/3$	$e^2/2$	$8/3$
B	$b-a/RT$	$b-a/RT$	$b-a/RT^2$
C	b^2	$b^2-ab/RT+a^2/2R^2T^2$	b^2

The law of corresponding states

Although all fluids give isothermals of the same general shape as fig. 1.2 the isothermals of different fluids do not, of course, coincide if plotted on the same diagram. To obtain the liquid–vapour part of the diagram for nitrogen for example, one must make measurements below 126°K, the critical temperature for nitrogen, while for xenon one may work up to 290°K, the critical temperature for xenon. One may ask, however, whether the behaviour of nitrogen at, say, one-half its critical temperature is similar to the behaviour of xenon at one-half its critical temperature. To make the meaning of this state-ment more precise we may introduce new measures of temperature pressure and volume called reduced measures. The reduced tempera-ture is a pure number T_r defined as the ratio of the actual tempera-ture of a fluid to its critical temperature, and similarly for reduced pressure p_r and reduced volume V_r:

$$T_r = \frac{T}{T_c} \qquad p_r = \frac{p}{p_c} \qquad V_r = \frac{V}{V_c} \qquad \text{2.9}$$

Instead of plotting p against V for various values of T one then plots p_r against V_r for various values of T_r. In this way different fluids can be accommodated on the same diagram. In particular, the critical points for all fluids have the same coordinates, namely $p_r = 1$, $V_r = 1$. The isothermals below the critical have values of T_r less than unity, those above greater than unity.

When this is done it is found that, generally speaking, the corresponding reduced isothermals of different substances do indeed nearly coincide. The agreement is not exact but is sufficiently close to warrant the following statement, which is known as the Law of Corresponding States: 'If any two of the reduced quantities p_r, V_r, T_r have the same value for a number of different substances then the third will also have very nearly the same value.'

The Law of Corresponding States applies most closely to fluids whose molecules are of the same nature, such as the group of the inert gases, or a group consisting of simple organic molecules of a non-polar character. Further discussion of it will be postponed till the nature of intermolecular forces and the statistical mechanical theory of fluids has been developed. Meanwhile it is of interest to show that the Law can be deduced from any equation of state that contains only three constants such as the a, b and R appearing in the van der Waals, Berthelot and Dieterici equations. We may, for example, write van der Waals' equation in terms of the reduced quantities by putting $p = p_r p_c = p_r(a/27b^2)$, $V = V_r V_c = V_r 3b$, $T = T_r T_c = T_r(8a/27Rb)$. On substituting these in the equation we find that a, b and R can be cancelled through in the various terms, leaving finally $(p_r + 3/V_r^2)(3V_r - 1) = 8T_r$. This is known as the reduced form of van der Waals' equation. If we substitute particular values for, say, V_r and T_r we obtain a unique value for p_r. Putting, for example, $V_r = 3$ and $T_r = \frac{1}{2}$ we obtain $p_r = \frac{1}{6}$. As the reduced equation contains no constants characteristic of a particular fluid this result is true for all fluids and is equivalent to the Law of Corresponding States.

To be able to write any equation of state in reduced form one must be able to eliminate the constants which appear in it. To do this one has the three equations which determine the critical data in terms of these constants. If the number of constants is greater than three, as in Clausius' equation, a reduced form cannot be obtained and so the Law of Corresponding States is not deducible. That the law is not exactly obeyed, is itself sufficient to show that no three-constant equation can represent accurately the p–V–T data for all fluids. Nevertheless, the fact that the inert gases, for example obey, the principle with remarkable accuracy shows that the nature of the intermolecular interactions must be closely similar for this group. We shall see later that the law can be deduced provided that the equation relating the force between a pair of molecules is of the same mathematical form for the different fluids and contains only two constants characteristic of a particular fluid.

Much of our knowledge of the law of force between molecules comes from the study of gases under conditions where they depart only slightly from ideal behaviour, that is, at moderately low densities. Under these conditions one may express the equation of state in the form of a simple power series such as

$$\frac{pV}{RT} = 1 + \frac{B}{V} + \frac{C}{V^2} + \frac{D}{V^3} + \cdots \qquad 2.10$$

where the quantities B, C, D... are functions of temperature, or alternatively one may write

$$\frac{pV}{RT} = 1 + B'p + C'p^2 + D'p^3 \ldots \qquad 2.11$$

These are called virial equations of state, and B, C, D, etc. (or B', C', D', etc.), are the virial coefficients. For an ideal gas the virial coefficients (except the first, which is unity) are all zero. The magnitudes of the virial coefficients therefore depend on the nature of the forces between molecules, whence the name (Latin *vis*, pl. *vires* = force). At large volumes or low pressures the successive terms diminish rapidly in numerical value. Greatest interest therefore attaches to the first few coefficients and particularly the second virial coefficient B (or B') and the rigorous theory[2] of slightly imperfect gases has been developed so far as to permit the calculation of this coefficient and its temperature variation for any reasonably simple law of force. It is of some interest therefore to see what predictions the empirical equations of state make about these coefficients.

To obtain, say, van der Waals' equation in virial form one first rearranges it as

$$p = \frac{RT}{V-b} - \frac{a}{V^2} \qquad 2.12$$

or

$$\frac{pV}{RT} = \frac{V}{(V-b)} - \frac{a}{RTV} = \left(1 - \frac{b}{V}\right)^{-1} - \frac{a}{RTV} \qquad 2.13$$

Providing b is less than V one may expand the bracket by the binomial theorem to give

$$\frac{pV}{RT} = 1 + \frac{b}{V} + \frac{b^2}{V^2} + \frac{b^3}{V^3} + \cdots - \frac{a}{RTV} \qquad 2.14$$

On comparing with 2.10 the virial coefficients are seen to be

$$B = b - \frac{a}{RT} \qquad C = b^2 \qquad D = b^3, \quad \text{etc.}$$

Similar procedures may be applied to the other equations. The virial coefficients B and C for these equations are given in table 2.2.

From experiments on imperfect gases it is found that the second virial coefficient is negative at low temperatures, becomes positive at higher temperatures, reaches a maximum and then decreases. (For all gases except hydrogen and helium the maximum in B lies at such high temperatures that accurate measurements are not possible.) The van der Waals expression for B gives, correctly, a negative B for low temperatures and a positive value at high temperatures. The maximum in the second virial coefficient is not, however, predicted by van der Waals' equation.

The range of validity of the virial expansion is limited by the convergence of the series. At high densities, of the order of liquid densities, the series diverges. At low and moderate densities, where the expansion is of use, very precise compressibility measurements are required to obtain accurate values of the virial coefficients, particularly the third and higher coefficients.

Phenomena in the critical region

At the critical point there is a nice balance between the molecular attractive forces, which tend to produce aggregation of the molecules into groups or clusters, and the disruptive effect of collisions, which tend to disperse these clusters. Raising or lowering the temperature by a fraction of a degree is sufficient to upset this balance severely. Marked changes are then observed in the behaviour of the fluid.

In 1863 Andrews described the behaviour of carbon dioxide in these words:[3]

On partially liquefying carbonic acid by pressure alone and gradually raising at the same time the temperature to 88° Fahr the surface of demarcation between the liquid and gas became fainter, lost its curvature and at last disappeared. The space was then occupied by a homogeneous fluid, which exhibited, when the pressure was suddenly diminished or the temperature slightly lowered, a peculiar appearance of moving or flickering striae throughout its entire mass.

Up to about one degree below the critical temperature the boundary surface between liquid and vapour is sharply defined and the density of the fluid changes abruptly from the liquid value to the vapour value as the boundary is crossed. Within a few tenths of a degree of the critical temperature the transition region becomes more diffuse and the variation of density with height is then more gradual. Very near the critical point the situation is complicated by the hydrostatic pressure gradient arising from the action of gravity on the column of fluid. Let z denote distance measured vertically upward in a column of unit cross-sectioned area in a fluid of density ρ. Consider a thin horizontal slice of fluid of unit area, and thickness dz. The mass of fluid in this slice is $\rho\,dz$ and the gravitational force on it is $\rho g\,dz$, acting downwards. This is balanced by the difference in pressure, dp, on opposite faces of the slice, acting upwards. We then have

$$-dp = \rho g\,dz \quad \text{or} \quad \frac{dp}{dz} = -\rho g \qquad 2.15$$

showing that the pressure decreases with height. In liquids and gases under ordinary conditions the corresponding variation of density with height over the dimensions of the container is negligible. At the critical point, however, the slope of the critical isothermal is zero and is very small in the immediate neighbourhood (fig. 1.2). A very small increase in pressure will therefore produce a large decrease in the volume, or a correspondingly large increase in the density. The density of a fluid near the critical point therefore decreases with increasing height in a continuous manner. This accounts for the lack of a sharply-defined boundary.

Figure 2.2 shows this variation in density for methyl ether[4] just below its critical temperature. The width of the transition region is seen to be roughly 4 cm.

By making some crude assumptions one may obtain, from the observed variation of density, a rough estimate of the size of the molecular clusters in a fluid. Consider first of all an ideal gas of molecular weight M. For one mole of gas we have

$$\frac{pV}{M} = \frac{RT}{M} \qquad 2.16$$

M/V is the mass of gas in volume, V, that is, the density, ρ, so that

$$p = \frac{\rho RT}{M} \qquad 2.17$$

In an isothermal column of gas, then

$$\frac{\mathrm{d}p}{\mathrm{d}z} = \frac{\mathrm{d}\rho}{\mathrm{d}z} \cdot \frac{RT}{M} \qquad 2.18$$

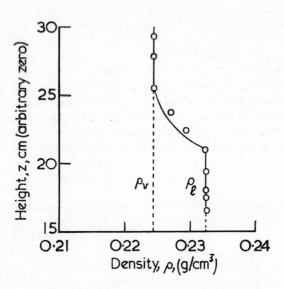

Fig. 2.2   Variation of density of methyl ether with height near the critical temperature. ρ_ℓ and ρ_v are the liquid and vapour densities and the solid line is calculated on the assumption that the molecular clusters contain $1{\cdot}8 \times 10^7$ molecules

whence, using eq. 2.15,

$$\frac{\mathrm{d}\rho}{\rho} = -\frac{Mg}{RT}\,\mathrm{d}z \qquad 2.19$$

Integrating this gives Halley's formula for the variation density with height:

$$\rho = \rho_0 \exp\left(-\frac{Mgz}{RT}\right) \qquad 2.20$$

where ρ_0 is the density at any convenient datum level, $z = 0$. This formula can be applied, for example, to determine the variation of density of the earth's atmosphere with height.

Now assume that in the critical state there are clusters of molecules all of the same size. These clusters may be regarded as independent giant 'molecules' of large 'molecular weight'. An equation analogous to Halley's formula can again be derived with a similar but much more rapid exponential decrease of density with height in the transition region. The effective 'molecular weight' of a cluster can then be found and hence the number of actual molecules it contains. For methyl ether under the above conditions this number is of the order of twenty million.

Critical opalescence

As the critical point is approached, from below or from above the critical temperature, the fluid loses its transparency and exhibits the milky shimmering appearance observed by Andrews. This is known as critical opalescence and is due to fluctuations in the density of the fluid over very small distances, distances comparable with the wavelength of light. For an ordinary gas or liquid these fluctuations are insignificant and the medium is optically homogeneous and transparent. In the critical region the fluctuations are much greater, an effect we may regard as due to the presence of the clusters. The medium is then optically non-homogeneous and a beam of light is scattered in all directions, giving the milky appearance. Critical opalescence is observed when the diameter of the clusters is of the same order of magnitude as the wavelength of light, say 6×10^{-5} cm, that is, a few hundred molecular diameters. The detailed theory of the scattering of light in the critical region is extremely complex[5] but estimates of cluster size obtained from light-scattering experiments agree approximately with estimates obtained from the variation of density with height.

Measurement of the critical constants[6]

Of the three critical constants the critical temperature is relatively easy to measure. A thick-walled glass tube is partially filled with pure liquid, all air is excluded and the tube sealed. On raising the temperature of a suitable thermostat in which the tube is kept, one of three things may happen. If too little liquid has been put in, the liquid level in the tube will fall to the bottom as the liquid evaporates and the tube will contain only unsaturated vapour before the critical

2

temperature is reached. If, on the other hand, too much has been put in, the level will rise as the liquid expands and will fill the tube below the critical temperature. The quantity of liquid must be adjusted by trial so that the density at the critical point will be approximately equal to the critical density. The meniscus will then disappear somewhere near the middle of the tube and the critical temperature can in this way be located to within about one-tenth of a degree. This heating at constant volume can be represented by a vertical line drawn upwards in the p–V diagram from a point on an isothermal in the liquid–vapour mixture region. Because the critical isothermal is very flat near T_c it is of little consequence if some error is made in filling; the meniscus can still be made to disappear within the tube.

The critical pressure may be obtained by using a tube sealed at the upper end only and transmitting the pressure, via mercury, to a suitable manometer. The critical pressure is also insensitive to changes in density and so can be accurately measured.

The critical density, ρ_c, is difficult to obtain by direct measurement, for the reasoning above applies in reverse to this quantity. Minute changes in pressure produce large changes in density along the critical isothermal. The critical density may, however, be obtained to within about one per cent by using the Law of Rectilinear Diameters, discovered by Cailletet and Mathias in 1886. The densities of the liquid, ρ_l, and the vapour, ρ_v, are measured over a range of temperature of about 20°C below the critical temperature. A graph of the arithmetic mean of these densities, $(\rho_l + \rho_v)/2$, against temperature is found to give a straight line. This is the rectilinear diameter (fig. 2.3). The diameter is produced to cut the vertical line through T_c at a point where $\rho_l = \rho_v = \rho_c$. If the range of temperature is too large the diameter may not be exactly linear over all its length.

The densities of the liquid and vapour may be measured by suspending a quartz sphere on the lower end of a quartz spiral spring in one or the other. The extension of the spring gives the effective weight of the sphere. By Archimedes' principle this effective weight depends on the buoyancy of the fluid, whose density can therefore be calculated.

The caloric equation of state

The caloric equation of state relates the total molecular energy of a fluid, U, to its volume and temperature. The molecular energy is the sum of the kinetic and potential energies of the molecules. For an ideal gas the energy is entirely kinetic and depends only on the temperature and not on the volume. In a real gas or liquid there is, in addition, potential energy due to the intermolecular forces, which depends on the average molecular separation. If we change this average distance by changing the volume the intermolecular forces do work (internal work) and so, in general, the potential energy of a fluid depends on the volume as well as on the temperature.

For simplicity let us consider a monatomic fluid. It may be shown

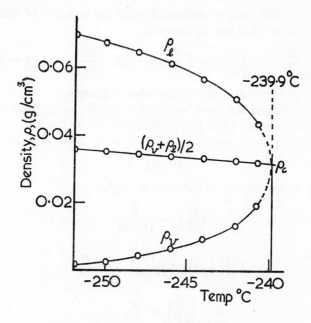

Fig. 2.3   The rectilinear diameter for hydrogen.
$T_{\rm c} = -239 \cdot 9°{\rm C}$, $\rho_{\rm c} = 0 \cdot 032$ gm cm^{-3}

that, whatever the volume, the molecular kinetic energy has the same value as that of the ideal gas, $\frac{3}{2}RT$. We may therefore write for the total internal energy,

$$U = U_{\rm kin} + U_{\rm pot} = \tfrac{3}{2}RT + U_{\rm pot}(V, T) \qquad 2.21$$

It is clearly of interest to know something of the relative magnitudes of the kinetic and potential energies. These we can estimate when the caloric equation of state is known. We can, however, relate the caloric equation of state of fluids to the ordinary equation of state, as follows.

Suppose we allow our fluid to expand isothermally by a volume δV. This will change the internal energy by an amount δU. The ratio of these changes in the limit is given by $(\partial U/\partial V)_T$. It is shown in text-books on thermodynamics that

$$\left(\frac{\partial U}{\partial V}\right)_T = T\left(\frac{\partial p}{\partial T}\right)_V - p \qquad\qquad 2.22\dagger$$

so that $(\partial U/\partial V)_T$ can be calculated when the equation of state is known. For an ideal gas, for example,

$$p = \frac{RT}{V} \qquad T\left(\frac{\partial p}{\partial T}\right)_V = T\frac{R}{V} = p \quad \text{and} \quad \left(\frac{\partial U}{\partial V}\right)_T = p - p = 0$$

confirming that U does not change when V changes.

Let us take van der Waals' equation as giving a rough description of the behaviour of a real fluid. Solving it for p we find

$$p = \frac{RT}{(V-b)} - \frac{a}{V^2} \qquad\qquad 2.23$$

a and b do not depend on temperature so that

$$\left(\frac{\partial p}{\partial T}\right)_V = \frac{R}{(V-b)}$$

and

$$T\left(\frac{\partial p}{\partial T}\right)_V - p = \frac{RT}{(V-b)} - p = \frac{a}{V^2}$$

Thus

$$\left(\frac{\partial U}{\partial V}\right)_T = \frac{a}{V^2} \qquad\qquad 2.24$$

For a finite change in volume along an isothermal we can integrate this equation to give

$$U = -\frac{a}{V} + \phi(T)$$

The function of temperature, $\phi(T)$, must be added in accordance

† For a small reversible expansion $T\,dS = dU + p\,dV$. Dividing by dV and keeping T constant gives $T(\partial S/\partial V)_T = (\partial U/\partial V)_T + p$. The Maxwell relation $(\partial S/\partial V)_T = (\partial p/\partial T)_V$ then gives 2·22.

with the rules of integration of partial derivatives. Along an isothermal T is constant so $\phi(T)$ is also constant and corresponds to the constant of integration for ordinary derivatives.

We can determine $\phi(T)$ for a monatomic fluid by noting that, as the volume becomes infinite, the fluid will behave as an ideal gas. If we denote the internal energy under this condition by U_∞ we have

$$\phi(T) = U_\infty = \tfrac{3}{2}RT \quad \text{(monatomic fluids)} \qquad 2.25$$

The caloric equation of state then becomes

$$U = -\frac{a}{V} + \tfrac{3}{2}RT \qquad 2.26$$

The two terms give, respectively, the magnitudes of the potential and kinetic energies. The internal energy is taken to be zero when the molecules are at rest at infinite separations.

Let us estimate the magnitudes of these energies for one mole of argon under various conditions. From the measured critical constants we find $a = 1\cdot345$ (litre)^2 atm mole^{-2}. If we express the volume V in litre mole^{-1}, the units of a/V are atm litre mole^{-1}. One atm litre is a unit of energy equal to $101\cdot3$ joules. With $R = 8\cdot32$ joules deg^{-1} mole^{-1} the internal energy in joules is given by

$$U = -\frac{136}{V\,(\text{litre})} + 12\cdot5T\,(^\circ\text{K}) > \text{joules mole}^{-1} \qquad 2.27$$

The table below shows the magnitudes of the potential and kinetic energy contributions for argon in various states.

TABLE 2.3

State	T°K	V (litres)	U_{pot} joules	U_{kin} joules	U joules
Gas N.T.P.	273	22·4	−6·1	3420	3414
Vapour N.B.P.	87·3	6·79	−20	1090	1070
Critical	150·7	0·0752	−1810	1885	75
Liquid N.B.P.	87·3	0·0287	−4750	1090	−3660

(N.B.P. = Normal Boiling Point)

From these figures we see that when the molecules are far apart, as in the gas or vapour, most of the energy is kinetic. The small numerical magnitude of the potential energy shows that, under these conditions, argon departs but little from ideal gas behaviour. In the neighbourhood of the critical point the potential energy is comparable with the kinetic energy, and in the liquid the major part of the energy is potential energy.

Van der Waals' equation is only approximately valid so that the above values of the potential energy must be regarded as only very rough estimates. To obtain proper values we must return to eq. 2.22 and apply it to the experimentally determined isothermals. If we allow our liquid to expand at temperature T from a volume V to an infinite volume, we get

$$\int_V^\infty dU = U_\infty - U(V, T) = \int_V^\infty \left\{ T\left(\frac{\partial p}{\partial T}\right)_V - p \right\} dV \qquad 2.28$$

Suppose we begin with a saturated liquid under its own vapour pressure p_s and allow it to expand in our piston and cylinder apparatus. The expansion to infinite volume is accomplished in two stages. First, the liquid vaporises at constant pressure from the volume of the liquid V_1 to the volume of the saturated vapour V_v. The contribution to the integral in this stage is

$$U_v - U_1 = \int_{V_1}^{V_v} \left\{ T\left(\frac{\partial p_s}{\partial T}\right)_V - p_s \right\} dV \qquad 2.29$$

As T, p_s and $(\partial p_s / \partial T)_V$ are constant during this stage (the last is the slope of the vapour pressure curve at T, which does not depend on volume) the integral is

$$U_v - U_1 = T\left(\frac{\partial p_s}{\partial T}\right)_V (V_v - V_1) - p_s(V_v - V_1) \qquad 2.30$$

This contribution may be calculated in another way. During the expansion heat must be supplied to vaporise the liquid, equal to the latent heat, L, and work of expansion is done by the piston against the external pressure, equal to $p_s(V_v - V_1)$. The change in internal energy is the difference of these quantities (First Law of Thermodynamics, ch. 5):

$$U_v - U_1 = L - p_s(V_v - V_1) \qquad 2.31$$

Comparing these two expressions for the internal energy change we see, incidentally, that

$$\left(\frac{\partial p_s}{\partial T}\right)_V = \frac{L}{T(V_v - V_1)} \qquad 2.32$$

a formula well-known in thermodynamics as the Clausius–Clapeyron equation.

For liquids at temperatures well below the critical this vaporisation process contributes by far the largest amount to the internal energy change. The further expansion of the unsaturated vapour to infinite volume:

$$U_\infty - U_v = \int_{V_v}^{\infty} \left\{ T\left(\frac{\partial p}{\partial T}\right)_V - p \right\} \mathrm{d}V \qquad 2.33$$

contributes only a small addition if the vapour is nearly ideal and can be estimated from a suitable equation of state, for example, a virial equation, which accurately represents the compressibility data of the vapour. On adding equations 2.31 and 2.33 we obtain $U_l - U_\infty$. The value of $U_l - U_\infty$, that is, the potential energy of liquid argon at the normal boiling point, calculated in this way, is -5840 joules mole^{-1}, which may be compared with the figure -4750 joules mole^{-1} obtained from van der Waals' equation.

The value of U_∞ for other gases are obtainable from the theory of ideal gases. For monatomic gases U_∞ is simply the kinetic energy of translation of the molecules, equal to $\frac{3}{2}RT$. For diatomic and polyatomic molecules there are additional contributions due to the rotations and vibrations of the molecules. These contributions require quantum mechanics for their calculation and fall outside the scope of this book.[7] Broadly speaking, the results are that, for diatomic molecules of the permanent gases at ordinary temperatures the rotational kinetic energy contributes an extra amount RT, but the vibration contribution is negligible. For hydrogen below about 50°K the rotational contribution is absent. We may take it that the value of U_∞ is accurately known for all simple molecules. Thus the value of U for a liquid at any volume and temperature—the caloric equation of state—can be determined from experimental measurements of latent heats, vapour pressures, etc.

From the molecular viewpoint the calculation of the ordinary and caloric equations of state of a liquid from a knowledge of the intermolecular forces can be regarded as a central objective of the theory of liquids. When these two equations are known many of the properties of a fluid in equilibrium—the so-called equilibrium properties—can be derived. Such properties are, for example, the coefficient of volume expansion, the isothermal compressibility and the specific heats at constant volume and constant pressure. Their relation to the two equations of state and to other thermodynamic properties are given in ch. 5.

The difference in any property of a real fluid at a certain volume and temperature and that of an ideal gas at the same volume and temperature arises because of the intermolecular forces. It is this difference which is of greatest interest to the theoretician. Our next objective is to see how molecules in a liquid are arranged in space and how this arrangement affects the calculated properties. Properties which depend on this arrangement or *configuration* are called configurational properties; the potential energy of the liquid, for example, is a configurational property. Molecular configurations in a liquid are best approached through a study of the arrangement in the solid state of the substance, where the molecules are in a regular geometrical pattern.

3

LIQUIDS CONSIDERED AS DISORDERED SOLIDS

At temperatures near the triple point (or effectively the normal melting point) the outstanding feature common to liquids and solids is the closeness of packing of the molecules. Taking once more the heavier inert gases as examples of the simplest kind of matter, the increase in volume when the solid melts at the triple point is only 15%.

The distinguishing feature between solids and liquids lies in the molecular arrangement. At the absolute zero of temperature, according to classical physics, the molecules in a crystalline solid are at rest in a regular geometrical pattern or space lattice. If the crystal is perfect this arrangement extends right throughout the solid up to the surface and crystalline solids are therefore said to exhibit long-range order. It is the existence of this lattice structure which gives to solids their rigidity.

If the temperature of the solid is raised, energy is communicated to the molecules. Two effects result from this. First, thermal expansion of the solid occurs. This we may regard as due to the expansion of the lattice as a whole, so that the distance between the lattice points increases. Secondly, the molecules no longer remain motionless, but vibrate about the rest positions, and the amplitude of this vibration increases with increasing temperature. Nevertheless, the mean positions still preserve a regular geometrical arrangement so that the long-range order is still maintained. To a first approximation the vibration of a molecule may be regarded as simple harmonic motion, in three dimensions, about the rest position. It must be remembered, however, that the actual forces determining the motion of a molecule arise from its neighbours and not from a restoring force originating at the rest position, and that these neighbours are also in motion. Thus the mathematical treatment of molecular motion in solids is by no means a simple problem.

If the temperature is raised still further the amplitude of the vibration becomes even greater until at a certain sharply-defined temperature the motion becomes so violent that the ordered lattice structure breaks down abruptly. This is the phenomenon of melting.

At any temperature we therefore again have a competition between the intermolecular forces, whose effect is to tend to produce an orderly arrangement, and the kinetic energy of the molecules, which tends to destroy this arrangement. If an external pressure is applied to the solid the usual effect is to increase the tendency towards order, that is, to favour the crystalline arrangement, and to counteract this tendency the temperature must be raised. Thus the melting point in general increases with increase in pressure, though water exhibits the opposite behaviour.

Above the melting point one may say that disorder triumphs over order. The victory is not, however, a total one. The tendency to form a regular lattice is still present in the liquid. If we fix our attention on a particular molecule the immediate neighbours will not be grouped around it in a completely random manner but in an arrangement which preserves some resemblance to the arrangement in the solid. The next nearest neighbours will show a much smaller degree of order with respect to our chosen molecule and at somewhat greater distances there will be no correlation at all between the position of any molecule and our chosen one. Liquids are therefore said to exhibit short-range order only. The distance over which this short-range order extends is of the order of a few molecular diameters. If the temperature of the liquid is raised the distance over which the short-range order is significant is reduced. The absence of long-range order in a liquid gives it the characteristic property of fluidity.

An alternative approach, then, to the study of a liquid is to regard it as in many respects similar to the highly-disordered solid. The first step is to find some mathematical way of representing the short-range order in liquids. This is accomplished by introducing the concept of a Radial Distribution Function.

Radial distribution functions in solids and liquids
The radial distribution function specifies the number of atoms or molecules to be found at any distance, *r*, from an arbitrarily chosen

molecule. If we consider first a perfect crystal at absolute zero, this number is determined by the geometrical structure of the lattice. Most monatomic solids crystallise in simple lattices of cubic or hexagonal symmetry. The inert gases, except helium, crystallise in the close-packed or face-centred cubic (c.c.p.) lattice in which eight atoms occupy the corners of a cube with six more at the centre of each face. Helium crystallises (under pressure) in a hexagonal close-packed (h.c.p.) lattice. The alkali metals crystallise in a body-centred cubic (b.c.c.) lattice in which one atom at the centre of a cube is surrounded by eight others at the corners. In an extended crystalline arrangement there is, however, no geometrical distinction in the spatial location of atoms. In the b.c.c. lattice, for example, any atom may be regarded as being at the centre of one cube or at one corner of another, as a study of a three-dimensional model of a crystal will make apparent.

As an example of the radial distribution function of a solid at absolute zero let us take the b.c.c. lattice of sodium. If we choose any atom as the origin atom we may regard it as the centre atom of a cube, surrounded by eight others. The shortest distance between one atom and its nearest neighbours is then one-half the diagonal of the cube. Let us call this distance a; for sodium it is 3·67 Å. The next-nearest neighbours are six in number, they all lie at a distance of $2a/\sqrt{3}$ from our original atom (at the centres of the neighbouring cubes) and so on for more distant atoms. Thus the atoms in any kind of lattice may be located on a series of spherical surfaces, centred on the chosen atom, whose radii bear simple numerical relationships to a determined by the geometry of the lattice.

Table 3.1 gives the number, N_r, of atoms to be found at any distance r from any arbitrarily chosen central atom (or molecule) for various simple lattice structures. The radii, r, in this table are expressed as multiples of the nearest-neighbour distance a. Also shown is the relation between a and the volume, V, occupied by N molecules, that is, the volume per molecule, which can be calculated from the lattice geometry.

The number of nearest neighbours, in the first shell, is called the coordination number of the lattice; it will be noticed that it is greatest (12) for the face-centred cubic and hexagonal close-packed lattices. These lattices have also the smallest volume per molecule, that is, the greatest density of packing.

A diagram in which N_r is plotted against r represents the radial distribution function for a solid at absolute zero. Figure 3.1(a) is the diagram for the b.c.c. lattice, the N_r are shown as a number of vertical lines.

Suppose now the crystal is not at absolute zero. Because of the molecular vibrations we cannot then regard the molecules as being located exactly on spherical surfaces. Instead we may enquire how many molecules are to be found within a spherical shell lying between r and $r + \delta r$ measured from the rest position of the central molecule. Let us denote this number by $g(r)\,\delta r$. A plot of the function $g(r)$ is shown in fig. 3.1(b). The vertical lines are now broadened into sharply-peaked curves, which increase in width as the temperature

TABLE 3.1

Number, N_r, of molecules in successive shells as function of shell radius r

	LATTICE TYPE						
	Body-centred cubic (b.c.c.)		Face-centred cubic (c.c.p.)		Hexagonal close-packed (h.c.p.)		Simple cubic
Shell No.	$(r/a)^2$	N_r	$(r/a)^2$	N_r	$(r/a)^2$	N_r	$(r/a)^2$ N_r
1	1	8	1	12	1	12	1 6
2	$1\frac{1}{3}$	6	2	6	2	6	2 12
3	$2\frac{2}{3}$	12	3	24	$2\frac{2}{3}$	2	3 8
4	$3\frac{2}{3}$	24	4	12	3	18	4 6
5	4	8	5	24	$3\frac{2}{3}$	12	5 24
etc.							
Volume per Molecule, V/N	$\frac{4}{3\sqrt{3}}a^3$		$\frac{1}{\sqrt{2}}a^3$		$\frac{1}{\sqrt{2}}a^3$		a^3

rises. The long-range order, however, is still reflected in the orderly spacing of these curves along the r-axis. The area under any peak will be equal to the number of molecules on the corresponding spherical surface of the original undisturbed lattice.

The radial distribution function for the liquid is shown in fig. 3.1(c). Here the long-range order has been entirely lost. At large radial distances the number of molecules whose centres lie between r and $r + \delta r$ is simply proportional to the volume of the spherical shell included between these limits. If $\rho_0 = N/V$ is the average number–density of the liquid as a whole, this number is $\rho_0 4\pi r^2 \delta r$. Hence at large distances $g(r)$ approaches $4\pi r^2 \rho_0$ and so is proportional to r^2. This gives the parabolic curve shown dotted in fig. 3.1(c). The full curve gives the actual distribution in a liquid and the short-range order is revealed by the departure of this curve from the dotted curve. This full curve starts from zero at a distance approximating to the 'diameter' of the molecule, rises to a maximum at a distance corresponding to the shell of the nearest neighbours, and shows smaller

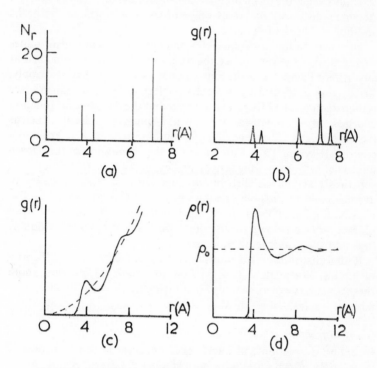

Fig. 3.1 Distribution functions for sodium (a) N_r for solid, $T=0°K$ (b) $g(r)$ for solid, $T>0°K$ (c) and (d) $g(r)$ and $\rho(r)$ for liquid

deviations from the dotted curve at slightly greater distances before the short-range order becomes finally lost.

An alternative way, therefore, of representing the structure of a liquid is to plot the number–density of the molecules $\rho(r)$ for any distance r. This is simply the number of molecules per unit volume at distance r and is again obtained by dividing the number in a spherical shell by the volume of the shell, that is

$$\rho(r) = \frac{g(r)\,\delta r}{4\pi r^2\,\delta r} = \frac{g(r)}{4\pi r^2} \qquad 3.1$$

The graph of this function is shown in fig. 3.1(d). At large distances $\rho(r)$ approaches the mean number–density for the liquid as a whole, ρ_0. At small distances the short-range order is revealed in the peaks and hollows of the full curve.

The distribution functions $g(r)$ and $\rho(r)$ represent mean values averaged over the time, since the number of molecules in a shell at any instant fluctuates as the molecules move about. They also apply, strictly, only to spherically symmetric molecules. No direction in space is then distinguished from any other so that the distribution function depends only on the distance r. For non-spherical molecules, such as the flat hexagon of benzene, the distribution function, if referred to a coordinate system fixed with respect to the orientation of the chosen molecule, will be a function of angles as well as r. To obtain a spherically symmetric distribution function it is then necessary to average over all possible orientations of the chosen molecule. The distribution functions obtained experimentally by X-ray and neutron diffraction (see below) are the ones which result from these double time and space averaging processes.

Radial distribution functions play a fundamental role in theories of liquids. Fortunately, it is possible to obtain information about these functions experimentally by studying the X-ray diffraction patterns of liquids.

X-ray diffraction in solids and liquids

In optics, diffraction and interference phenomena can be produced in a variety of ways and have been studied for over a century and a half. In particular, interference phenomena can be observed whenever a beam of light falls on a body having a regular or periodic structure. One way of producing such a structure is to rule with a diamond a large number of parallel and equally-spaced lines on a glass plate, to give a diffraction grating.

When a parallel beam of monochromatic light falls normally on the plate most of the light issuing from the plate goes straight on but, if the spacing between the lines is very small, a number of much less intense beams are observed to emerge at certain angles to the undeviated beam. These are the diffracted rays. Each unruled space in the grating may be regarded as a source of secondary waves which spread out in all directions. Because of the wave nature of light, however, these secondary waves tend to annul each other by destructive interference. Only in the directions where they can reinforce each other will diffracted rays be found. If the angle which a diffracted ray makes with the undeviated beam be θ the condition for reinforcement is

$$d \sin \theta = n\lambda \quad (n = 1, 2, 3, \text{etc.}) \qquad 3.2$$

where d is the distance between adjacent rulings and λ the wavelength of the light. Of the set of diffracted rays corresponding to the various values of n the most intense is usually that corresponding to $n = 1$, which is called the first-order diffracted ray.

From the above equation we may deduce a simple requirement for the successful observation of diffraction phenomena which applies in general. If the diffracted rays are to be observed they must make a reasonably large angle with the primary beam. This means that d and λ must be of the same order of magnitude. For visible light λ is of the order of 10^{-5} cm, hence the rulings must be very closely spaced.

In 1912 it occurred to Professor Max von Laue that, if the arrangement of molecules in a crystal is a regular one, it ought to be possible to observe diffraction phenomena. A crystal differs in two respects from the diffraction grating. First, the arrangement of atoms in a crystal is three-dimensional rather than the two-dimensional arrangement of lines on the grating. Secondly, the spacing between adjacent atoms is about one thousand times less than for the rulings on a grating. In order to observe diffraction in crystals, therefore, one must use radiation whose wavelength is about one thousand times less than 10^{-5} cm, that is, about 10^{-8} cm, or 1 Å. This radiation lies in the X-ray region of the electromagnetic spectrum.

In the famous experiment of Laue and his collaborators, Friedrich and Knipping, a narrow beam of X-rays was allowed to fall on a crystal of zinc blende (zinc sulphide). To detect the X-rays a photographic plate was placed on the other side of the crystal. When the plate was developed an intense central black spot was found, produced by the undiffracted ray, surrounded by a regular geometrical pattern of weaker spots. This regular pattern produced by the diffracted rays proved that the molecules in a crystal are arranged in an orderly manner, and since 1912 X-ray diffraction has become a powerful tool for the investigation of the structure of crystals. Mathematical methods were quickly developed which enabled the type of crystal structure and the lattice spacings to be calculated from the arrangement and spacing of the spots on the diffraction photograph.

After von Laue's discovery experiments were quickly made by Friedrich in 1913 and by Debye and Scherrer in 1916 to see what diffraction patterns, if any, a liquid will produce. The diffraction pattern of a liquid is not nearly as striking as that of a crystal. Instead of a pattern of sharply defined spots a liquid produces only one or two weak diffuse rings surrounding the intense central spot. This lack of sharpness reflects the lack of long-range order in liquids. The diffuse rings do, however, show that some regularity of structures exists in a liquid. They confirm the existence of short-range order.

In the very early experiments on X-ray diffraction the primary beam contained a number of rays of different wavelengths. To investigate X-ray diffraction phenomena quantitatively a primary beam of a single wavelength, that is a beam of monochromatic X-rays, must be used. With a copper target in the X-ray tube the characteristic K_α line of copper ($\lambda = 1.54$ Å) may be employed. Unwanted radiation of other wavelengths is removed by suitable thin metal foil filters, or by a preliminary diffraction of the beam by a crystal (crystal monochromator). The liquid under observation may be contained in a thin-walled tube, or the beam may be allowed to impinge directly on the free surface of the liquid, which avoids the complication introduced by the scattering produced by the walls of the tube. The free-surface method cannot be used for very volatile liquids or for, say, chemically reactive metals at high temperatures which tend to form oxide layers on the surface. The diffracted beams may be recorded on a photographic plate but, because the beams are so weak, long exposures are necessary. In recent years the Geiger counter has tended to replace the photographic plate as a more sensitive detector, the number of counts per unit time being proportional to the intensity of the diffracted beam. A counter provides direct and fast observation, and unwanted X-rays can be discriminated against by suitable electronic circuits. Several thousand counts must be recorded at each angular setting of the counter with respect to the incident beam in order to reduce the error arising from random statistical fluctuations in the counting rate. In addition to these statistical fluctuations the output of the X-ray tube is liable to vary over the period of the experiment. This does not matter in the photographic method as all parts of the pattern are equally affected. In the counter method the output of the tube is monitored by a second counter, fixed in position, and arranged so as to receive a small proportion of the incident beam. Suitable corrections can then be made to the observations.

From a diffraction experiment is obtained the intensity, I_s, of the diffracted rays as a function of the angle, θ, between the incident and diffracted beams. It is then possible to deduce the radial distribution function by a method first worked out by Zernicke[1] and Prins in 1927. Each molecule in the liquid scatters the incident beam. If one molecule be chosen as the reference molecule, the interference of beams scattered by its neighbours will depend on the distances and positions of these neighbours with respect to it, that is, on $\rho(r)$. By averaging over all directions and over all radial distances from the reference molecule, an expression for the intensity of the diffracted beam at an angle θ is obtained in which the unknown radial distribution function $\rho(r)$ appears under an integral sign. By means of a mathematical theorem known as Fourier's inversion theorem this formula can be transformed so that $\rho(r)$ is given by an integral of the diffracted intensity. The final result for monatomic liquids is

$$\rho(r) = \rho_0 + \frac{1}{2\pi^2 r} \int_0^\infty \left[\frac{I_m}{I_s} - 1 \right] s \sin(sr) \, ds \qquad 3.3$$

in this equation the variable of integration s is related to the angle of diffraction θ by the equation

$$s = \frac{4\pi}{\lambda} \sin \frac{\theta}{2} \qquad 3.4$$

I_m/I_s is the ratio of the intensity which would be obtained at an angle θ in the absence of short-range order to the actual intensity. The value of I_m can be obtained by observing the scattering in the vapour of the liquid at low densities where the molecules are so far apart that the interference of the scattered beams of different molecules is negligible. The quantity I_m is, effectively, the diffracted intensity of a single molecule, and is itself a complicated quantity, since X-rays are scattered by all the electrons in the molecule. For simple molecules with a few scattering electrons I_m may be calculated theoretically, but generally it must be determined by experiment.

When I_m and I_s are known, the integral in the above equation may be evaluated by graphical or numerical methods. Thus the value of $\rho(r)$ can be obtained at various radial distances.

The radial distribution curve for liquid argon is shown in fig. 3.2, taken from the observations of Eisenstein and Gingrich.[2] The ordinates of the curves are the ratios of $\rho(r)$ to ρ_0, so that at large values of r the curves approach unity. Along the abscissa is plotted the ratio (r/σ) where the distance σ is 3·42 Å. σ is the parameter which appears in the Lennard–Jones potential function (p. 62); it may be regarded

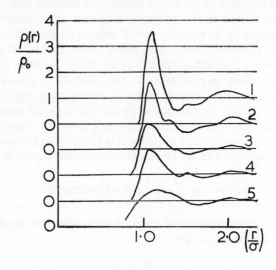

Fig. 3.2   Radial distribution function for liquid argon at points
on the saturated liquid curve (1) 84·4°K (2) 91·8°K (3) 126·7°K
(4) 144·1°K (5) 149·3°K

as an approximation to the 'diameter' of the argon atom. For the sake of clarity the ordinates of all curves, except No. 1, have been displaced vertically.

The curves reveal how the short-range order is gradually lost as the temperature is increased. Curve 1 is for the triple point, 84·4°K, while curve 5 is for 149·3°K which is virtually the critical point (150·7°K).

The heights of the first maxima show that at the triple point the number–density of the immediate neighbours of the central atom is over three times the value for the liquid as a whole and falls to about one and a half times the mean density near the critical point. Secondary maxima and minima visible near the melting point become blurred or lost at the higher temperatures. The finer details of experimentally determined radial distribution functions are, however, very sensitive to experimental and computational errors and it is likely that some of the smaller peaks have no real existence.

Neutron diffraction

The radial distribution functions of liquids may also be obtained from neutron diffraction experiments. Because of the dual wave-particle nature of matter a neutron of mass m moving with a velocity v will behave in certain respects as a wave of wavelength λ given by de Broglie's relation $\lambda = h/mv$, where h is Planck's constant. The procedure is similar to that of X-ray diffraction. A beam of low velocity (thermal) neutrons obtained from an atomic pile is first diffracted from a single crystal of lead or copper so as to give a monochromatic beam of wavelength about $1 \cdot 1$ Å. This beam then falls on the liquid and the scattered intensity is measured by a proportional counter filled with boron tri-fluoride. Neutrons are scattered by the nuclei of atoms so that complications may arise if the liquid contains an element with more than one isotope, since the isotopes vary in their scattering powers. On the other hand, neutrons are scattered by light elements (hydrogen helium, etc.) for which X-ray scattering is negligible. Several hundred[3] investigations of the structure of liquids, both simple and complex, have now been carried out by X-ray and neutron diffraction methods.

The glassy state[4]

We saw in ch.1 that some substances, like ordinary glass, do not seem to be unambiguously classifiable as either solid or liquid. At sufficiently high temperatures they flow like ordinary liquids but if progressively cooled they do not crystallise at a sharply defined temperature, their flow simply becomes more and more sluggish until, at a sufficiently low temperature, they can be regarded for all intents and purposes as rigid solids. Although our main concern in this book will be with the very simple types of liquid which do not show this behaviour, the properties of glasses are very instructive in revealing the importance of configurational structure, or short-range order, in all liquids.

One of the early surprises in X-ray diffraction experiments was the discovery that glasses give the diffuse-ring pattern characteristic of liquids even down to the lowest temperatures. We must conclude, therefore, that glass, even though in a solid-like state, nevertheless preserves a disordered atomic arrangement. The explanation of how this can happen is to be found in the phenomenon of supercooling.

As is well known, it is possible, with care, to cool many ordinary liquids somewhat below their normal freezing temperature without solidification. Small quantities of water, free from dust or other nuclei, if slowly cooled in smooth-walled vessels can be supercooled some 10 or 20°C. Such supercooled liquids, however, are generally very unstable and will readily crystallise on further cooling, or if agitated. They will always do so very rapidly if inoculated with a small particle of the crystalline solid, which acts as a nucleus for crystal growth.

The glasses form a class of substances which can be supercooled very easily, so easily that it is often difficult to induce crystallisation to occur at all. We will extend the term 'glass' to cover the wide range of substances which have this property and it includes, besides ordinary glass, pure silica, glycerine, glucose and other sugars (when boiled and cooled these give the hard glassy solids familiar to the toffee maker), rubber and the wide range of plastics. Some of these, like ordinary glass, are of complex chemical composition, others, like silica and glycerine, are pure compounds.

The feature which distinguishes the glasses from ordinary liquids is their abnormally high viscosity in the region of the freezing point (or liquidus temperature, in the case of the compound bodies). In order to crystallise, a nucleus must be able to form in the supercooled liquid and this means that at least a small number of molecules must move and rotate so as to arrange themselves in a regular pattern. If the viscosity is high and the molecule of a complicated shape, with strongly directional intermolecular forces, it is plausible to infer that this nucleation process is strongly hindered or, if it does occur here and there, that the subsequent rate of crystal growth is greatly reduced. The viscosity of all liquids increases very rapidly with decrease of temperature so that if a highly viscous liquid is cooled, not too slowly, molecular rearrangements or configurational changes are rapidly brought virtually to a standstill and the disordered configuration becomes 'frozen in'. At sufficiently low temperatures the viscosity becomes so high that viscous flow becomes undetectable, even over long periods of time. This is the glassy state, which we may therefore define as the state of a supercooled liquid of extremely high viscosity.[5]

Because glasses have the molecular structure of a liquid but the external appearance of a solid, their properties are full of interest both to the pure scientist and the practical man who has to use them. The lack of a crystalline structure explains, for example, why glasses show a typical conchoidal fracture pattern rather than the characteristic cleavage planes of crystalline solids.

For our brief study of their physical behaviour we may take as a typical glass-forming substance glycerine (glycerol) which, chemically, is a tertiary alcohol of formula CH_2OH—$CHOH$—CH_2OH. The normal freezing point of glycerol is 17·9°C, at which temperature its viscosity is about 17 poise, or about 1000 times the viscosity of water at its freezing point. Hence glycerol readily supercools and at low temperatures becomes a hard glassy solid very similar to ordinary glass.

Many physical properties of a glass, such as the specific heat, the thermal expansion coefficient, the index of refraction and the dielectric constant, if measured over a wide temperature range, show a marked change in their magnitude over a rather sharply defined temperature interval. This interval may be only a few degrees and so can be approximately specified by a temperature, T_g, called the glass transformation temperature. For glycerol the behaviour of the specific heat, which is typical of the general pattern, has been investigated by Simon and Lange[6] and is shown in fig. 3.3. Over a small range of temperature near 180°K the specific heat decreases to about half its value. The above properties of other glasses show similar phenomena, the value of T_g being characteristic of the particular glass. For polystyrene they occur near $T_g \sim 350°K$, ordinary silica glass $T_g \sim 800°K$ and pure silica $T_g \sim 1500°K$.

The explanation of this behaviour is obtained from an observation by Tammann that the viscosity of any glass at T_g is always in the neighbourhood of 10^{13} poise (such high viscosities require special methods of measurement). The significance of this particular figure can be qualitatively explained by simple arguments based on the method of dimensions.

If we apply a shear stress to a crystalline solid, a static elastic deformation or shear strain occurs, the stress and strain being related by the shear, or rigidity, modulus, n. A shear stress applied to a liquid, on the other hand, gives a steady viscous flow at a rate determined by the viscosity coefficient, η. In the glassy state we can, by suitably adjusting the temperatures, observe both processes; an elastic strain appears when the stress is first applied, followed by viscous flow, with partial recovery of the strain when the stress is removed. This led Maxwell to suggest that viscous flow in any liquid could be interpreted as the continued breakdown of an elastic strain. If we suppose

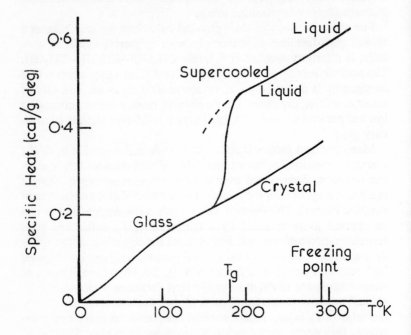

Fig. 3.3   The specific heats of crystalline and supercooled glycerol

that both strain and flow are always present their relative importance can therefore be qualitatively indicated by the magnitude of the ratio η/n. By dimensional analysis this ratio is found to have the dimensions of a time and if η and n are both in c.g.s. units this time will be in seconds.

Now an inspection of a table of physical constants shows that for most solids n does not vary greatly from one to another, or with temperature, and is commonly of the order of 10^{11} c.g.s. units. As the densities of solids and liquids do not differ greatly we may suppose that the strength of the intermolecular forces in liquids approximates to that in solids so that the shear moduli of liquids, could we but measure them, would be found to be of the same order. For ordinary liquids the viscosity rarely exceeds 10^{-2} c.g.s. units (poise) so that η/n is of the order of 10^{-13} seconds. This means that the breakdown of elastic deformation in liquids—or as we would now say, the changes in the molecular configuration—occur so rapidly as to be beyond detection. For a glass at its transformation temperature, however, where $\eta \sim 10^{13}$ poise the ratio η/n is of the order of seconds or minutes. Changes in the configuration, induced by external stresses or other experimental operations, will therefore require a time for their effective completion which, at T_g, will be comparable with the duration of the measurement process itself. If we lower the temperature by some 10 degrees or so the viscosity may increase by several orders of magnitude so that η/n becomes of the order of days or weeks, and over the duration of the experiment we may say that the configuration will remain virtually unaltered. T_g therefore is the temperature which, for most practical purposes, marks the 'freezing in' of the molecular configuration.

With this idea we are able to explain the specific heat curve for glycerol. With some difficulty glycerol, kept just below the normal melting point, can be persuaded to crystallise, so that at any lower temperature Simon and Lange could make measurements on both the crystalline and glassy forms. For liquids a major contribution to the specific heat comes from change in intermolecular potential energy due to the variation of the configuration with temperature, so that above T_g the specific heat curve of the supercooled liquid exceeds that of the crystal and, moreover, joins smoothly on to the curve for the ordinary liquid at the melting point. Below T_g this configurational contribution drops out leaving only a contribution from the vibrational motion of the molecules about fixed points. This contribution is similar in nature and numerical magnitude for the crystal and the glass, the distinction being merely that of the geometrical arrangement of the fixed points—lattice-like in the crystal, disordered in the glass. In the vicinity of T_g itself the measured values depend on the duration of the experiment, if extended over a longer period of time a greater contribution from the slowly changing configuration will be obtained. By waiting a long time before taking readings Oblad and Newton[7] were, in later experiments, able to follow the dotted curve a little way below T_g. The other physical properties of glasses which depend on configuration changes can be interpreted in a similar manner.

Many aspects of the manufacture and technology of ordinary glass can be guided by the above ideas. If we raise the temperature well above T_g, so that configurational change can take place fairly quickly, there is always a danger that crystallisation may begin, which in glass is called devitrification. An experienced glass-blower knows that he must not keep glass in the flame for too long; if he does it may devitrify, the mass of tiny crystals giving the glass an opaque frosted appearance; devitrified glass is of such poor mechanical strength as to be useless. Fused quartz is particularly liable to devitrification, which is readily initiated by specks of dust on the surface, so that a glass-blower will always scrupulously clean quartz before working it.

Again, glasses which have high expansion coefficients, if cooled too rapidly from a temperature well above T_g to well below, will be in a state of severe mechanical strain, which the almost completely frozen configuration cannot relieve. Slow changes over a long period of time, while possibly relieving strain in one part, may then build it up at another so that the article may fracture, spontaneously and explosively, perhaps many years later. To prevent this, a manufacturer will anneal the glass by maintaining it for a long time in the vicinity of T_g and then cooling it slowly to room temperature.

From the point of view of thermodynamics the behaviour of glasses raises many far-reaching problems, since a glass below T_g is not in a state of thermodynamic equilibrium, at least with respect to the crystalline solid. We have met states of meta-stable equilibrium before, in superheated liquids and supersaturated vapours, but these meta-stable states are precarious and easily recognisable, so that there is no difficulty in bringing the system to the true equilibrium state. A glass well below T_g cannot be induced to crystallise, so that thermodynamic reasoning must be applied to glasses only with great care.

For the liquids of low viscosity with simple molecules, to which we now return, the glassy state is unobtainable and we can apply thermodynamic arguments in full confidence that they refer to states of true thermodynamic equilibrium.

4

THE NATURE OF INTERMOLECULAR

FORCES IN LIQUIDS

Let us imagine we have two molecules separated by a distance r with no other molecules nearby. For the moment we shall suppose that the force exerted on one molecule by the other acts along the line joining them. We adopt the usual convention that attractive forces are given a negative sign and repulsive forces a positive sign. The general way in which the force, $F(r)$, varies with the separation is shown in fig. 4.1(a). At large distances the force is attractive but changes to a repulsion at short distances which increases very rapidly with further decrease in r.

In discussing the properties of matter the energy concept is a much more powerful tool than the concept of force. We therefore plot in fig. 4.1(b) the mutual potential energy, $\phi(r)$, of the molecules as a function of r. The relation between $F(r)$ and $\phi(r)$ is that the work done in producing a small increase in r, that is, $F.dr$, is equal to the decrease in the mutual potential energy, $-d\phi$, or

$$F(r) = \frac{-d\phi(r)}{dr} \qquad 4.1$$

so that the slope of the $\phi(r)\_r$ curve with the sign changed gives the magnitude of the force. The potential energy is, by convention, chosen to be zero when the molecules are separated by an infinite distance.

At the minimum in the $\phi(r)$_r curve, $d\phi(r)/dr=0$, so that the value of r, say $r=r_0$, at which this minimum occurs marks the change from attraction to repulsion. This distance, of the order of an Ångstrom unit or so, would be the equilibrium distance between a pair of isolated undisturbed molecules. The depths of the minimum is the energy required to separate such a pair and so is a measure of the strength of the binding forces. From general considerations we would expect that strongly-bound substances will form relatively hard

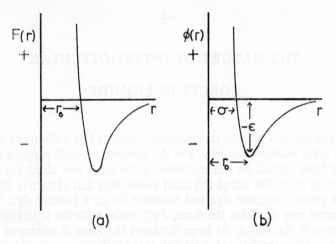

Fig. 4.1   The variation with separation of (a) the force (b) the
mutual potential energy of a pair of molecules

solids with high melting and boiling points and large latent heats of fusion and vaporisation.

Molecular physics seeks for the origin of the attractive and repulsive forces in the electronic structures of atoms and molecules, and such studies[1] enable us roughly to classify the forces into four types, depending on the nature of the attractive or binding component. These are (a) valence binding, (b) ionic binding, (c) metallic binding and (d) van der Waals binding. Of these four, the types of binding called valence, exhibited for example by diamond, and ionic, exhibited by common salt, are so strong that the substances are solid at ordinary temperatures, so these types of binding are of little interest to us. Metals are bound together by forces which depend on the presence of free electrons, able to move through the solid as a whole. This binding may vary greatly in strength, as is shown by the great range of melting points of metallic elements, from $-39°C$ for mercury up to $3370°C$ for tungsten. The theory of this type of binding is complex and difficult.

The fourth type of binding, the van der Waals binding, is the type chiefly responsible for the cohesion of those substances which exist as liquids at or below ordinary temperatures. The nature of the binding force in these substances is relatively easy to understand and is the one in which we shall be chiefly interested. These substances can be readily obtained as gases or vapours, and as the imperfection of gases, due to these forces, was first studied by van der Waals the name given to this type of binding is explained.

The molecules of this group may be further divided into polar and non-polar. When two or more atoms are chemically bound together to form a molecule the originally spherically-symmetric electron distribution round the atoms is distorted. This distortion may give the molecule a permanent electric moment so that, at any rate to a first approximation, it may be visualised as a permanent electric dipole, that is, as equivalent to a pair of equal and opposite charges $\pm q$ separated by a distance x. The electric moment, μ, of such a dipole is given by $\mu = qx$. When, for example, a hydrogen atom combines with a chlorine atom to form a molecule of hydrogen chloride, HCl, there is a displacement of the electronic structure towards the chlorine atom. The molecule therefore behaves as though this end had an excess negative charge and the hydrogen end a positive charge and so the molecule is polar. If we take q as of the order of one electronic charge, 4.8×10^{-10} e.s.u., and the effective shift, x, as of the order of a fraction of an Ångstrom unit, 10^{-8} cm, the dipole moment comes out as of the order of 10^{-18} e.s.u. $\times$ cm, known as the Debye unit. The dipole moment of hydrogen chloride is, in fact, 1.08 Debye units. This is, however, a relatively large moment; most molecules have smaller moments. In carbon monoxide, CO, the moment is only 0.12 Debye units, the oxygen being the negative end.

Whether a molecule has a permanent dipole moment or not will depend on the symmetry of the atomic configuration. Diatomic molecules in which the two atoms are of different elements (heteronuclear molecules) will exhibit electronic distortion to a greater or lesser degree and will therefore be polar. If the two atoms are identical, as in N_2 or O_2, we have a homo-nuclear molecule and these are non-polar, since there is no reason for the electron structure to be displaced towards one atom rather than the other. All monatomic elements, for example the inert gases, are necessarily non-polar, as are all symmetrical molecules. Methane, CH_4, is non-polar, hence the four hydrogen atoms must be symmetrically disposed about the carbon atom. They are, in fact, at the corners of a regular tetrahedron with the carbon at the centre. If one, two or three of these hydrogen atoms are replaced by chlorine atoms the symmetry is destroyed and a polar molecule results, but if all four are replaced we have the symmetrical and non-polar molecule of carbon tetrachloride.

It must be remembered that, while the dipole moment of a molecule is a perfectly real and measurable quantity, the representation of a polar molecule as two point charges separated by a distance x is only a convenient model. We shall use such a model, however, for the purposes of calculation since our final formulae can be written in terms of the dipole moments or other measurable quantities. A further simplification may be made if we assume that the separation x can be decreased and the charge q increased indefinitely in such a way as to keep their product constant, so that the formulae appropriate to 'short' dipoles may be used (as in elementary electrostatics and magnetism). Such a dipole is known as a point dipole. This simplification introduces some error into our final formulae if the distance between the dipoles is small but, as a first approximation, this error may be neglected.

Induced dipoles

When a molecule is in an electric field the positive atomic nucleus and the negative electrons are subjected to forces in opposite directions. The resulting distortion of the electronic structure gives rise to a dipole known as a field-induced dipole, or simply an induced dipole which, in contrast to a permanent dipole, disappears when the field is removed. Induced dipoles may be produced in any molecule, whether polar or non-polar, and to distinguish them we shall, where necessary, denote the induced dipole by μ_i and any permanent dipole by μ_p.

The simplest assumption that can be made about the induced dipole, and one that proves to be adequate, is that the induced dipole moment is proportional to the electric field strength, E, or

$$\mu_i = \alpha E \qquad\qquad 4.2$$

where the constant α is a measure of the ease of deformation of the electronic structure by the field and is known as the polarisability of the molecule. This equation is analogous to Hooke's Law in elasticity, the distortion (or strain) being taken as proportional to the field (or force). In non-spherical molecules the polarisability may vary with the orientation of the molecule with respect to the field, and in such cases we may suppose α to represent an average value over all orientations.

The field E may be a man-made one, for example, that between the plates of a charged condenser, or it may arise from the near presence of a polar molecule. In the latter case it gives rise to a force between the molecules which, for any mutual orientation, is always an attractive one. The situation is very similar to that which gives rise to the attractive force between a permanent magnet and a piece of soft iron. The field of the magnet induces a magnetic moment in the iron which leads always to an attraction between them, no matter what the orientation of the magnet axis.

The orders-of-magnitude of the potential and field near a polar molecule can be estimated as follows. From elementary electrostatics the potential, V, and field, E, at a point distant, r, from the centre of a point dipole and lying on the axis (the 'end on' position) are given by

$$V = \frac{\mu_p}{r^2}, \qquad E = \frac{2\mu_p}{r^3} \qquad \qquad 4.3$$

Take, for example, a point 3 Å from an HCl molecule, regarded as a point dipole of moment $1 \cdot 08 \times 10^{-18}$ e.s.u. The potential is

$$\frac{1 \cdot 08 \times 10^{-18}}{(3 \times 10^{-8})^2} = 1 \cdot 2 \times 10^{-3} \text{ e.s.u.}$$

and the field

$$\frac{2 \times 1 \cdot 08 \times 10^{-18}}{(3 \times 10^{-8})^3} = 8 \cdot 0 \times 10^4 \text{ e.s.u.}$$

To convert to practical units we use the relation 300 volts = 1 e.s.u. The potential is then 0·36 volts and the field strength 24 million volts per cm. An atom of, say, argon, of polarisability $\alpha = 1 \cdot 6 \times 10^{-24}$ cm^3, placed in this field would develop an induced dipole moment $\mu_1 = \alpha E = 1 \cdot 6 \times 10^{-24} \times 8 \times 10^4$ e.s.u. $= 1 \cdot 3 \times 10^{-19}$ e.s.u., or 0·13 Debye units.

When two molecules are close together their mutual potential energy will be due to the following distinct causes. If both molecules are polar there will be a potential energy due to the interaction of their permanent dipoles. We shall call this the electrostatic energy ϕ_s. Secondly, there will be a contribution due to the interaction of the dipole induced in each molecule with the permanent dipole of the other. This is the induction energy, ϕ_i. Finally, there is a third contribution whose origin is not immediately apparent, known as the London or dispersion energy ϕ_d. The explanation of the origin of this energy we shall leave till later.

To a good approximation these three contributions to the total energy can be treated separately and added to give the total energy, that is $\phi(r) = \phi_s + \phi_i + \phi_d$, and these three contributions we now proceed to investigate in more detail.

The electrostatic energy

Suppose for simplicity that the axes of the dipoles are collinear. The dipoles are regarded as point charges $\pm q_1$ and $\pm q_2$ separated by distances x_1, x_2, so that $\mu_1 = q_1 x_1$ and $\mu_2 = q_2 x_2$. Let the distance between the positive charges be r, fig. 4.2. As the mutual potential

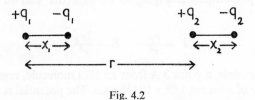

Fig. 4.2

energy of two charges q_1, q_2 separated by a distance d is $q_1 q_2/d$ the mutual potential energy for this special orientation, which we denote by ϕ'_s, is the sum of similar expressions for pairs of charges in different molecules, that is

$$\phi'_s = \frac{q_1 q_2}{r} - \frac{q_1 q_2}{(r - x_1)} - \frac{q_1 q_2}{(r + x_2)} + \frac{q_1 q_2}{(r + x_2 - x_1)} \qquad 4.4$$

or

$$\phi'_s = \frac{q_1 q_2}{r}\left\{1 - \left(1 - \frac{x_1}{r}\right)^{-1} - \left(1 + \frac{x_2}{r}\right)^{-1} + \left(1 + \frac{[x_2 - x_1]}{r}\right)^{-1}\right\} \qquad 4.5$$

When x_1 and x_2 are less than r we may expand the various terms by the binomial theorem. All terms up to the second order then cancel, except for the product term from the square bracket giving

$$\phi'_s = \frac{-2q_1q_2x_1x_2}{r^3} + \text{higher order terms}$$

or

$$\phi'_s = \frac{-2\mu_1\mu_2}{r^3} \qquad 4.6$$

in the limit when the dipoles become point dipoles. The negative sign indicates that the molecules attract each other. If, however, we turn one dipole through 180° we obtain a positive energy and a repulsion between the dipoles. In the general case where the dipole axes are not collinear the potential energy depends on the mutual orientations being positive for some and negative for others. As we may expect that, at any rate in gases, the molecules are in constant rotation, it might appear at first sight that the average potential energy and force would be zero. This, however, is not so, as we shall see later (ch. 5) the probability of a particular orientation depends on the potential energy, those of a low potential energy being more favoured than those of a high energy in a manner governed by a proportionality factor $\exp(-\phi/kT)$. When due allowance is made for this, by averaging over all orientations suitably weighted, it is found that the average potential energy ϕ_s is always negative but falls off more rapidly with distance than ϕ'_s, being given by

$$\phi_s = \frac{-2\mu_1^2\mu_2^2}{3kTr^6} \qquad 4.7$$

or for identical molecules, $\mu_1 = \mu_2 = \mu_p$,

$$\phi_s = \frac{-2\mu_p^4}{3kTr^6} \qquad 4.8$$

In these expressions we have neglected terms of a higher order than $1/r^6$. The force is therefore one of attraction which weakens with increasing temperature.

The induction energy

The magnitude of the induction energy is readily obtained. As before, we consider first the special case of a point on the axis of a permanent dipole. The field, E, is $2\mu_p/r^3$. A second molecule at this point will develop an *induced* dipole moment $\mu_1 = \alpha E$, in the direction of the axis. The interaction energy, ϕ_i', is between this induced dipole and the permanent dipole is then given by a formula similar to 4·6 of the previous case, that is

$$\phi_i' = \frac{-2\mu_p\mu_i}{r^3}$$

Putting $\mu_i = \alpha E = \alpha . 2\mu_p/r^3$ gives

$$\phi_i' = \frac{-4\alpha\mu_p^2}{r^6} \qquad 4.9$$

In contrast to the previous case, however, it now makes no difference to the sign of this energy if the permanent dipole is turned through 180°, for this reverses also the direction of the induced dipole. The energy is thus negative for any orientation of the permanent dipole. The effect of this is that, when we average over all possible orientations with the weighting factor exp $(-\phi_i/kT)$, the inverse sixth power law is still retained, only the numerical constant being altered, moreover, to a first approximation, the average interaction energy is independent of the temperature. The total average induction energy for a pair of identical polar molecules is found to be given by

$$\phi_i = \frac{-2\alpha\mu_p^2}{r^6} \qquad 4.10$$

The London or dispersion energy
The electrostatic energy described above depends on the presence of a permanent dipole moment in both of the molecules. The induction energy only exists if at least one of the molecules is polar. If both molecules are non-polar there seems no reason why attractive forces should exist between them. A clue to the origin of the attractive forces which explains the cohesion of non-polar substances can be obtained from the following reasoning.

In a classical picture of an atom electrons are regarded as point charges in rapid motion about the positive nucleus. While, on average, the distribution of electrons is spherically symmetrical the instantaneous configuration of the electrons may be such as to give the atom an electric moment. This moment will polarise a nearby atom giving it an induced dipole and leading to an attraction between the two in a manner similar to the induction effect described above.

Such a picture of the electronic structure of free atoms is, however, quite untenable from the point of view of the quantum theory. To attempt to calculate the attractive force by classical electrostatics is quite unjustified in this case. Strictly speaking, of course, all intermolecular forces should be treated on a quantum mechanical basis, but the classical treatment is adequate for the electrostatic and induction effects. For this third contribution, however, quantum methods are essential, and were first fully developed by F. London[2] in 1930. Fortunately, a simple treatment of this effect on a quantum basis is possible which is instructive in revealing the origin of this force.

The motion of a particle describing a circle with uniform velocity may be regarded as compounded of two linear simple harmonic motions at right angles. Similarly, the three-dimensional motion of an electron about the nucleus of an atom may be resolved into three linear simple harmonic motions. Let us consider only one of these, along the x-axis, so arriving at the concept of a linear oscillator, that is, an electron of charge e and mass m vibrating as though it were bound to a fixed point by a restoring force $-kx$, proportional to the displacement.

The mechanical energy, w, of the oscillator is the sum of its potential energy $\frac{1}{2}kx^2$ and its kinetic energy $\frac{1}{2}mv^2$ or $\frac{1}{2}m\dot{x}^2$.

$$w = \tfrac{1}{2}kx^2 + \tfrac{1}{2}m\dot{x}^2 \qquad 4.11$$

The frequency, v_0, of the vibration is given by

$$v_0 = \frac{1}{2\pi}(k/m)^{1/2} \qquad 4.12$$

So far the treatment has been entirely classical. In classical physics all values of the energy are possible depending on the amplitude of the vibration. The characteristic feature of the quantum theory is that only certain values E_n of the energy are permitted and that these are related to the classical frequency by the equation

$$E_n = (n + \tfrac{1}{2})hv_0 \qquad 4.13$$

where $n = 0, 1, 2, 3$, etc. An atom will normally be in the lowest energy state, corresponding to $n = 0$, and given by

$$E_0 = \tfrac{1}{2}hv_0 \qquad 4.13(a)$$

This minimum energy is the zero-point energy, which has no analogue in classical physics.

3

Consider now two linear oscillators vibrating along the line joining them, the distance between the fixed points being r. If we place fixed positive charges at these points, numerically equal to the electronic charge, we have a model of two rapidly fluctuating dipoles whose interaction will represent the dispersion forces between molecules. If the instantaneous displacements of the electrons from the fixed points are x_1 and x_2 we obtain a diagram similar to fig. 4.2 and the mutual potential energy of the oscillators is given by an expression similar to the one worked out for that picture, i.e. $-2x_1x_2e^2/r^3$. The only difference is that x_1 and x_2 now vary harmonically with the time. The total energy, w, of the two oscillators is therefore partly mechanical and partly electrostatic and is given by

$$w = (\tfrac{1}{2}kx_1^2 + \tfrac{1}{2}m\dot{x}_1^2) + (\tfrac{1}{2}kx_2^2 + \tfrac{1}{2}m\dot{x}_2^2) - \frac{2x_1x_2e^2}{r^3} \qquad 4.14$$

The effect of the extra term is to change the frequencies of vibration by an amount which depends on the separation. Because of this term it is not immediately obvious how to get the new frequencies from the energy equation, but a simple change of variables enables these to be found. Introduce new coordinates x_+ and x_- related to x_1 and x_2 by the equations

$$x_+ = \frac{x_1 + x_2}{\sqrt{2}} \qquad x_- = \frac{x_1 - x_2}{\sqrt{2}} \qquad 4.15$$

Adding and subtracting these equations gives

$$x_1 = \frac{x_+ + x_-}{\sqrt{2}} \qquad x_2 = \frac{x_+ - x_-}{\sqrt{2}} \qquad 4.16$$

Similarly for the velocities, as $\dot{x}_1 = dx_1/dt$ etc., we get

$$\dot{x}_1 = \frac{\dot{x}_+ + \dot{x}_-}{\sqrt{2}} \qquad \dot{x}_2 = \frac{\dot{x}_+ - \dot{x}_-}{\sqrt{2}} \qquad 4.17$$

Putting these values of x_1, x_2, $\dot{x}_1$ and $\dot{x}_2$ in the energy equation we obtain

$$w = \frac{1}{2}\left(k - \frac{2e^2}{r^3}\right)x_+^2 + \frac{1}{2}m\dot{x}_+^2 + \frac{1}{2}\left(k + \frac{2e^2}{r^3}\right)x_-^2 + \frac{1}{2}m\dot{x}_-^2 \qquad 4.18$$

The advantage of the new variables is now clear. The equation contains no product term in these variables and the energy equation is similar in form to the energy equation for two non-interacting oscillators, but with different force constants. The new frequencies, ν_+ and ν_-, of these oscillators are

$$\nu_+ = \frac{1}{2\pi}\left(\frac{k-2e^2/r^3}{m}\right)^{\frac{1}{2}} \quad \text{and} \quad \nu_- = \frac{1}{2\pi}\left(\frac{k+2e^2/r^3}{m}\right)^{\frac{1}{2}}$$

or

$$\nu_+ = \nu_0\left(1-\frac{2e^2}{kr^3}\right)^{\frac{1}{2}} \quad \text{and} \quad \nu_- = \nu_0\left(1+\frac{2e^2}{kr^3}\right)^{\frac{1}{2}} \qquad 4.19$$

The new zero-point energy of the two oscillators is therefore

$$E_0' = \tfrac{1}{2}h\nu_+ + \tfrac{1}{2}h\nu_- \qquad 4.20$$

On substituting for ν_+ and ν_- and expanding the radicals by the binomial theorem as far as the squared terms this reduces to

$$E_0' = h\nu_0 - \frac{e^4 h\nu_0}{2k^2 r^6} \qquad 4.21$$

The term $h\nu_0$ is the sum of the zero-point energies of the uncoupled oscillators. The second term shows that there is an attractive energy between interacting oscillators which, with the neglect of the higher terms, varies as the inverse sixth power of their distance apart. This is the London, or dispersion, energy, ϕ_d.

The force constant, k, can be related to the polarisability of the oscillator by returning to the classical picture and considering the static displacement, x_s, of an electron in a steady field, E. This exerts a force Ee on the electron which is balanced by the restoring force kx_s. So $x_s = Ee/k$ and, as the induced dipole moment is $\mu_i = ex_s = \alpha E = e^2 E/k$, we have $e^2/k = \alpha$. The dispersion energy, ϕ_d, is then, from 4.21, equal to $-\alpha^2 h\nu_0/2r^6$.

To calculate the magnitude of ϕ_d for real molecules the simple treatment must be extended to the three-dimensional motion of an electron and the contributions of all electrons in the molecule added, each with its characteristic frequency ν_0. To estimate these frequencies we observe that ν_0 is related to the absorption spectrum of the molecule, for, in quantum theory, a linear oscillator can only absorb or emit radiation of frequency ν_0. A fuller treatment along these lines reveals that only the outermost electrons contribute significantly to the dispersion energy and that the value of $h\nu_0$ can be approximated to the ionisation energy of the molecule, E_i. The final expression for the dispersion energy is therefore little altered except for a change in the numerical constant and is given, though only as a fairly rough estimate, by

$$\phi_d = \frac{-3\alpha^2 E_1}{4r^6} \qquad \qquad 4.22$$

Relative magnitudes of the contributions to the van der Waals energy
The interaction energies for the three effects all vary as the inverse sixth power of the distance between the molecules, so their relative importance is determined by the coefficients of this quantity. To calculate them we require the dipole moments and polarisability of the molecules. These may be obtained from the refractive indices and dielectric constants of the gases. In table 4.1 is given some relevant

TABLE 4.1

van der Waals interaction energies

	$\mu \times 10^{18}$ e.s.u.	$\alpha \times 10^{24}$ cm^3	$h\nu_0$ eV	Electrostatic $r^6\phi_s \times 10^{60}$ erg cm^6	Induction $r^6\phi_i \times 10^{60}$ erg cm^6	Dispersion $r^6\phi_d \times 10^{60}$ erg cm^6
CO	0·12	1·99	14·3	0·0034	0·057	67·5
HI	0·38	5·4	12	0·35	1·68	382
HBr	0·78	3·58	13·3	6·2	4·05	176
HCl	1·03	2·63	13·7	18·6	5·4	105
NH$_3$	1·5	2·21	16	84	10	93
H$_2$O	1·84	1·48	18	190	10	47

data for a number of simple polar molecules at 20°C, taken from the work of London.[2]

It will be seen that the induction contribution is always small. The dispersion effect is always large and contributes the major part to the van der Waals energy, if the permanent dipole moment is less than about 1 Debye unit. In non-polar molecules only the dispersion effect exists, this effect therefore accounts for the cohesion of such non-polar substances as the inert gases.

The repulsive energy
In the modern picture of the atom the electrons are regarded as arranged in a series of concentric spherical shells about the nucleus.

The maximum number of electrons in each shell is strictly limited by a quantum mechanical rule, the Pauli Exclusion Principle, and this principle governs the repulsive forces between atoms.

When two atoms approach one another so closely that the outermost shells begin to overlap one of two things may happen. If the outermost shells do not have their full complement of electrons a mutual sharing of electrons may occur. The energy of the combination may then be much less than that of the separate atoms, giving a stable diatomic molecule bound by strong valence forces. If the outermost shells are full, as in the inert gases, the effect of bringing the atoms together is to force more electrons into the same region of space than the Pauli principle allows. The resultant distortion of the electron configuration appears as a strong force of repulsion, increasing very rapidly with decreasing distance. The calculation of the repulsive energy is a formidable problem, needing extensive and tedious calculations in even the simplest cases of atoms with few electrons, such as hydrogen and helium. Over limited ranges of r expressions obtained for the variation of repulsive energy, ϕ_R, with distance can be approximated to an exponential decrease of the form

$$\phi_R = A \exp -\frac{r}{r_1} \qquad 4.23$$

where A and r_1 are constants, r_1 being a characteristic length of the order of a fraction of an Ångstrom unit. Alternatively, the repulsion may be represented by a simple inverse power relationship of the form

$$\phi_R = \frac{c}{r^n} \qquad 4.24$$

where c and n are constants, whose values are best determined experimentally. For many simple substances the best value of n is in the neighbourhood of 12.

The total potential energy of a pair of molecules
Combining the repulsive and attractive contribution to the potential energy and taking the value of 12 for n, we arrive at an expression for the total potential energy of the form

$$\phi(r) = \frac{c}{r^{12}} - \frac{d}{r^6} \qquad 4.25$$

where c and d are constants. This is the Lennard–Jones function and is extensively used in the study of interactions of simple non-polar molecules. The term $-d/r^6$ then represents the dispersion energy. For weakly polar molecules this term may be taken as including also the electrostatic and induction effects. For strongly polar molecules a simple inverse power law is less satisfactory, as the assumption of free rotation of the molecules leads to a dependence of d on temperature. This assumption itself is allowable for gases but not for condensed states.

A plot of $\phi(r)$ against r gives a curve of the shape of fig. 4.1(b). The constants c and d may be written in terms of the energy $-\epsilon$ and either the distance r_0 or σ from the conditions

$$\phi = 0 \quad \text{at} \quad r = \sigma; \qquad \frac{d\phi}{dr} = 0 \quad \text{at} \quad r = r_0; \qquad \phi = -\epsilon \quad \text{at} \quad r = r_0$$

These give alternative, and more convenient, forms of 4.25 as

$$\phi(r) = \epsilon\left\{\left(\frac{r_0}{r}\right)^{12} - 2\left(\frac{r_0}{r}\right)^{6}\right\} \qquad 4.26$$

or

$$\phi(r) = 4\epsilon\left\{\left(\frac{\sigma}{r}\right)^{12} - \left(\frac{\sigma}{r}\right)^{6}\right\} \qquad 4.27$$

with $r_0^6 = 2\sigma^6$, that is, $r_0 = 1 \cdot 1224\sigma$.

The distance, σ, may be regarded as the 'diameter' of the molecules as the term is used in kinetic theory for, by the conservation of energy, it is the closest distance which two molecules attain in a head-on collision if they start far apart with negligibly small velocities.

For some purposes simpler expressions may be employed. In elementary kinetic theory a molecule is often represented as an infinitely hard non-attracting sphere of diameter σ, that is

$$\phi(r) = \infty, \quad r < \sigma; \qquad \phi(r) = 0, \quad r > \sigma$$

A more realistic model includes an attractive term added to the hard sphere core, for example

$$\phi(r) = \infty, \quad r < \sigma; \qquad \phi(r) = -d'/r^6, \quad r > \sigma$$

which is the type of model implied in the arguments used to 'derive' van der Waals' and other equations of state. Or the attractive forces may be represented by a 'square well' model, that is

$$\phi(r) = \infty, \quad r < \sigma; \qquad \phi(r) = -\epsilon', \quad \sigma < r < c'\sigma;$$
$$\phi(r) = 0, \quad r > c'\sigma$$

where ϵ' and c' are constants, with c' of the order of 1·50.

Determination of the constants in potential functions

Owing to the difficulties of an exact calculation of the magnitudes of the intermolecular interactions it is preferable to appeal to experiment to deduce numerical values of the constants. The two chief sources of information are the properties of slightly imperfect gases and of the crystalline solid at absolute zero. The properties of gases are determined by the interaction ('collision') of a pair of molecules, and rigorous theories exist for simple spherical molecules which relate the potential function to such properties as the second virial coefficient and viscosity. For an assumed law of interaction the values of the constants which best fit the data can then be found by trial.

The properties of the solid are determined by the simultaneous interaction of a number of molecules. It is therefore necessary to inquire whether the potential energy of a pair of molecules is affected by the presence of others. If not, the energies and forces are said to be additive, and the calculation of the total potential energy is greatly simplified. For simple chemically stable molecules it appears that the assumption of addivity introduces only a very small error, so that the total potential energy of an assembly of N molecules, Φ, may be written as a sum of terms, one for each pair of molecules, that is

$$\Phi = \sum_{\text{pairs}} \phi_{ij}(r_{ij}) = \sum_{i>j} \phi_{ij}(r_{ij}) = \frac{1}{2} \sum_{i=1}^{N} \sum_{j=1}^{N} \phi_{ij}(r_{ij}) \qquad 4.28$$

where $\phi_{ij}(r_{ij})$ is the mutual potential energy of molecules i and j and r_{ij} their separation. The three different ways of expressing Φ are all equivalent and ensure that the contribution of each pair is counted once only. With this understanding we shall usually employ the first expression.

For the crystal at absolute zero the molecules have (in classical physics) no kinetic energy. The total energy is then entirely potential energy and is equal to the energy required to separate the molecules to infinite distances from each other. This is the zero-point latent heat of sublimation, $L_{sub.}$ a quantity which can be derived from experiment.

To relate this to the constants in the potential function let us consider, say, an inert gas at 0°K which crystallises in a face-centred cubic lattice (c.c.p.). The potential energy of one atom, say i, relative to all the others may be obtained by placing i at the origin and summing the contributions of atoms in successive spherical shells, the number of atoms in any shell and its radius being known (table 3.1). This is repeated for each atom in turn chosen as the origin atom, giving just N times the result, but to obtain the total potential energy this value must be divided by two because the contribution of any pair i, j, has been counted twice, once when i was the central atom with j in a shell, and once for the reverse case. For the Lennard–Jones function the contributions of successive shells to the repulsive energy fall off rapidly, but the attractive contributions fall off much more slowly, the final result for the zero-point potential energy, Φ_0, being

$$\Phi_0 = \frac{N\epsilon}{2}\left\{12{\cdot}132\left(\frac{r_0}{a}\right)^{12} - 2(14{\cdot}454)\left(\frac{r_0}{a}\right)^6\right\} \qquad 4.29$$

which may be compared with 4.26. The numerical coefficients in 4.29 show that nearly all of the repulsive energy and about five-sixths of the attractive energy is due to the shell of the 12 nearest neighbours. From table 3.1 the distance a may be related to the volume of the crystal at 0°K, V_0; for the c.c.p. lattice for example $a^3 = \sqrt{2}V_0/N$.

To this classical energy, however, must be added a quantum correction, the zero-point energy of the crystal, K, which can be estimated from the quantum theory of specific heats. In Debye's theory this is given by $K = \frac{9}{8}Nk\theta_D$ where θ_D is the Debye characteristic temperature. The total internal energy of the crystal at 0°K, U_0, is then

$$U_0 = \Phi_0 + \tfrac{9}{8}Nk\theta_D = L_{sub} \qquad 4.30$$

The nearest-neighbour distance, a, must be such as to make U_0 a minimum. If the zero-point nearest neighbour distance is a_0 we have therefore

$$\left(\frac{\partial U_0}{\partial a}\right)_{a=a_0} = 0 \qquad 4.31$$

With this value of a the equations 4.30 and 4.31 may be solved to give the two unknowns ϵ and r_0, whence σ is also obtained from $r_0^6 = 2\sigma^6$.

In table 4.2 the constants σ and $T_0 = \epsilon/k$ for some simple molecules are given. Here k is Boltzmann's constant and T_0 has the dimensions of a temperature. The reason for expressing ϵ in this way rather than in ergs is as follows. As explained in ch. 2 a significant factor determining the state of a thermodynamic system is the relative magnitudes of the kinetic and potential energies. As the mean kinetic energy of a molecule at temperature T is of the order kT the equivalent temperature T_0 gives a convenient and illuminating measure of the depth of the potential well, ϵ, in the Lennard–Jones function.

TABLE 4.2

Constants in the Lennard–Jones 6–12 function[3]

	Ne	A	Kr	Xe	N_2	CH
σ (Å)	2·75	3·405	3·60	4·10	3·70	3·82
$\epsilon/k = T_0$, °K	35·6	119·8	171	221	95·1	148·2

5

THE FOUNDATIONS OF THE THEORY OF

LIQUIDS IN EQUILIBRIUM

We now turn to the problem of relating the measurable properties of a liquid in thermodynamic equilibrium to the law of force between its molecules. The mathematical methods for this task were built up mainly in the nineteenth century in the closely related sciences of Thermodynamics and Statistical Mechanics. We shall deal with these sciences only very briefly and so far as possible in a physical manner, referring the reader to other works[1] for more rigorous mathematical discussions of the formulae we obtain.

Thermodynamics is built on a foundation of three laws, of which only the first and second need concern us. The first law is the law of conservation of energy; it states that energy can neither be created nor destroyed but only converted from one kind to another. Of the many different kinds of energy thermodynamics is particularly concerned with heat energy, and energy which appears as useful work.

Let us return to our piston and cylinder and suppose it to contain unit mass (one gram molecule) of matter, at volume V, temperature T and pressure p. The state of the matter—whether solid, liquid or gas or a combination—is immaterial. Suppose now that a small quantity of heat δQ is supplied to the system, which is also allowed to expand by a volume δV. From the equation, work = force × distance, we find that the work, δW, done by the system is given by $\delta W = p \cdot \delta V$.

The first law then states that the heat energy supplied must be equal to the sum of the work done by the piston and the increase in the molecular energy, δU,

$$\delta Q = \delta U + \delta W = \delta U + p \cdot \delta V \qquad 5.1$$

So far we have considered only an infinitesimal change. We shall employ the symbol Δ to denote a finite change and so

$$\Delta Q = \Delta U + \Delta W = \Delta U + \int p \, dV \quad \text{(finite change)} \qquad 5.2$$

We now introduce the term 'thermodynamic state'. Hitherto, we have used the word 'state' to distinguish the solid liquid and gaseous forms of matter. In the thermodynamics of fluids the word has a different meaning. It means the values of pressure, volume temperature, etc., pertaining to a particular condition of thermodynamic equilibrium. Thus a 'change of state' means that a system moves from a condition where the pressure, volume, temperature, etc., have particular values to a condition where they have different values. It does not necessarily mean a melting or vaporisation process, which in thermodynamics is called a 'change of phase'.

A thermodynamic state may be represented graphically by choosing as ordinate and abscissa any two variables which serve to fix the state. If, for our piston and cylinder, we choose pressure and volume, we get an indicator diagram, an idea we owe to James Watt.

Suppose our device contains one mole of a fluid initially at pressure p_i and volume V_i (fig. 5.1). We may represent this state by the point i. If now the fluid is heated and allowed to expand it will reach a new final state, f, along a path represented by the full curve in the figure. Such a diagram provides an easy interpretation of the work done in the change. This is $\Delta W = \int_i^f p \, dV$ and the integral is represented by the area between the curve and the V-axis bounded by the ordinates at i and f.

The diagram helps to make clear a fundamental distinction between ΔU on the one hand and ΔQ and ΔW on the other. Although these quantities are all forms of energy (and one understood to be measured in the same units), ΔU is a change in a *property of the system* while ΔQ and ΔW are measures of *operations* or *processes* carried out on, or by, agencies external to the system. The internal energy, U, of our fluid has a definite (though possibly unknown) value which is fixed when the state of the system is fixed. This value does not depend on the previous history† of the fluid but only on its present state. If the state is changed from i to f, the new value of U will also be unambiguously fixed by the new coordinates and the nature of the transition process is immaterial. This fact is expressed by the statements 'U is a function of the state only' or 'the change in U is independent of the path taken'.

It is quite otherwise with the work ΔW. If, by varying the heat supply, we had changed the state from i to f by a different path, shown dotted in fig. 5.1, we should have obtained a different quantity of work, represented by the smaller area under the dotted curve. Indeed,

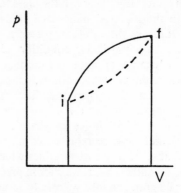

Fig. 5.1   Indicator diagram for an expansion process

by choosing different paths, we may obtain any quantity of work we please from the system. We express this by the statement: 'The work done is not a function of the state only, but depends on the path chosen.' Since $\Delta Q = \Delta U + \Delta W$ it follows that, as ΔW can have any value while ΔU has a fixed value, their sum, ΔQ, can also have any value. If ΔW is large ΔQ is large and conversely; their difference, ΔU, being always fixed and determined only by the initial and final values of p, V, T, etc.

It is the business of statistical mechanics to supply us with a means of calculating U for a system in any specified state. It turns out, however, that a knowledge of U only will not give us complete information about the measurable thermodynamic properties of the system. To obtain complete knowledge we need one more property. One

† This is not true of glasses.

such property, the entropy, we can define with the aid of the second law of thermodynamics.

We have seen that the heat supplied to the system depends on the path chosen and so is not a function of the state. The second law states that if we calculate the integral

$$\int_i^f \frac{\mathrm{d}Q}{T} = \Delta S \quad \text{(reversible process)} \qquad 5.3$$

where $\mathrm{d}Q$ is the small quantity of heat supplied in an infinitesimal change at temperature T, we shall obtain a result which is independent of the path connecting i and f, provided only that the change is carried out reversibly. For one path the absorption of heat may be large, but if so the temperature of the system, though it may vary continuously, will tend to be high. For another path the heat absorbed may be small, but this will be a path along which the temperature will tend to be low, and the value of the integral will be the same. This remarkable result permits us to define a new function of the state, the entropy, S. We define an infinitesimal increase in entropy by the equation

$$\delta S = \frac{\delta Q}{T} \quad \text{(reversible process)} \qquad 5.4$$

and a finite change, ΔS, by the above integral.

The word 'reversible' in the above definitions has, roughly speaking, its ordinary meaning of a process which can go as easily backwards as forwards. Thus there must be no frictional forces acting on our piston, so that if the system does a certain amount of work in going from i to f an exactly equal amount must be done on it to return it from f to i *along the same path*. Furthermore, the change must be imagined to be carried out slowly and in such a manner that the system at any instant differs only infinitesimally from an equilibrium state. Of course, all real processes are, strictly, irreversible because friction, heat losses, and the like can never be wholly eliminated, but it is possible to imagine some idealised experiments in which these irreversible effects are made vanishingly small.

So far we have defined only changes in the functions U and S. To give a definite numerical measure to these quantities we can choose any convenient reference state as a datum level. For fluids the most convenient reference state is that of the gas or vapour at temperature T and a volume which is so large that the gas can be regarded as ideal.

The internal energy and entropy of a fluid at the same temperature and any volume V can then be obtained from a reversible isothermal change of volume such as we have already employed in ch. 2.

The internal energy and entropy are less familiar concepts than those of pressure, volume, temperature, etc. These latter are most directly perceptible to the senses and are directly measurable by experiment. In attempting to explain the behaviour of matter, however, the less familiar quantities U and S prove to be most simply related to the molecular properties. The measurable properties, however, can always be obtained quite simply from either U or S. Indeed, by combining these two in a single new function of the state, all the thermodynamic properties of matter in equilibrium can be calculated from this one new function. This new function, the Helmholtz free energy F, is defined by the equation

$$F = U - TS \qquad\qquad 5.5$$

We can, in fact, show that F has the virtue of possessing a reasonably familiar physical meaning. Let us combine the first and second laws for an infinitesimal reversible process by eliminating δQ between equations 5.1 and 5.4. We obtain $T\,\delta S = \delta U + \delta W$. Let us further suppose this process is isothermal, so that T is constant. We may then put $T\,\delta S = \delta(TS)$ so that

$$\delta(TS) = \delta U + \delta W \quad \text{or} \quad \delta(TS - U) = \delta W$$

That is, using 5.5, $-\delta F = \delta W$. For a finite isothermal reversible change we get

$$-\Delta F = \Delta W \qquad\qquad 5.6$$

In words, this equation states that if any thermodynamic system undergoes any reversible isothermal process the work done is equal to the decrease in the free energy. In the special case of the piston and cylinder the work is work of expansion.

This interpretation of the function F explains the name 'free energy'. The word 'free' is, perhaps, unfortunate because of its everyday connotation of something for nothing, an idea which is anathema to the whole doctrine of conservation of energy. It is used here in the sense of 'available'. The free energy of a system is that part of the total internal energy U which is available as external work in an isothermal reversible process. The residue, TS, is the unavailable energy.

When the free energy is known as a function of volume and temperature, which we indicate where necessary by the notation $F = F(V, T)$, all the measurable thermodynamic properties can be obtained, as follows. For any reversible infinitesimal general change in F, not necessarily isothermal, we can write

$$\mathrm{d}F = \mathrm{d}(U - TS) = \mathrm{d}U - T\,\mathrm{d}S - S\,\mathrm{d}T \qquad 5.7$$

If only work of expansion is done we have also

$$T\,\mathrm{d}S = \mathrm{d}U + \mathrm{d}W = \mathrm{d}U + p\,\mathrm{d}V \qquad 5.8$$

Substituting for $T\,\mathrm{d}S$ in 5.7 we get

$$\mathrm{d}F = -p\,\mathrm{d}V - S\,\mathrm{d}T \qquad 5.9$$

For the special case in which T is constant, $\mathrm{d}T = 0$,

$$\left(\frac{\partial F}{\partial V}\right)_T = -p \qquad 5.10$$

which gives the pressure as a function of volume and temperature, that is, the equation of state. (We notice in this equation a characteristic feature of theoretical physics; a force-like quantity, the pressure, is obtained by differentiating an energy.) From the equation of state we can find the volume coefficient of expansion, β_T, by another differentiation because $\beta_T = (1/V)(\partial V/\partial T)_p$. The isothermal bulk modulus, B_T, can also be found, from $B_T = -V(\partial p/\partial V)_T$.

For another special case of equation 5.9 obtained by keeping the volume constant, $dV = 0$, we find

$$\left(\frac{\partial F}{\partial T}\right)_V = -S \qquad 5.11$$

which gives the entropy. Putting this expression for S back in the definition of F itself, eq. 5.5, gives,

$$F = U + T\left(\frac{\partial F}{\partial T}\right)_V \qquad 5.12$$

the important Gibbs–Helmholtz equation, which relates the free and internal energies without the explicit appearance of the entropy. As $F = F(V, T)$ the Gibbs–Helmholtz equation will relate U to V and T also, that is, it will give, for a substance in a single phase, the caloric equation of state. The specific heat at constant volume, C_v, is obtained from eq. 5.1 by putting $dV=0$ and dividing by dT,

$$C_v = \left(\frac{\partial Q}{\partial T}\right)_V = \left(\frac{\partial U}{\partial T}\right)_V \qquad 5.13$$

The specific heat at constant pressure, C_p, follows from a well-known thermodynamic relation,

$$C_p = C_v + T\left(\frac{\partial p}{\partial T}\right)_V\left(\frac{\partial V}{\partial T}\right)_p \qquad 5.14$$

The derivatives on the right-hand side can be calculated from the equation of state.

Thus the task of the theoretical physicist is reduced to calculating the functions U and S, or F, for a given system of molecules. The information at his disposal is a knowledge of the law of force between molecules and the number of molecules in the system, together with the volume of the system and its thermodynamic temperature. This task is the province of the science of Statistical Mechanics.

Statistical mechanics

The science of mechanics is concerned with the laws which govern the motion of matter in response to the forces which act on it. The fundamental laws which enable problems in mechanics to be solved for ordinary-sized bodies, such as cannon balls or pendulums, are Newton's famous laws of motion. In particular the second law, that the time rate of change of the momentum is proportional to the force, can be applied directly to solve problems in simple cases.

For more complicated motions more powerful mathematical methods are required. These were built up in the eighteenth and nineteenth centuries and are associated with the names of Laplace, Lagrange and Hamilton. Roughly speaking, these methods may be regarded as alternative formulations of the laws of motion in terms of the kinetic and potential energies of the moving bodies, rather than force. The advantage of energy concepts are, first, that energy is a scalar quantity while force is a vector. Scalars can be combined by simple algebraic addition while vectors must be combined by the parallelogram rule. Secondly, the law of conservation of energy can be called to the aid of the mathematician when necessary.

In attempting to apply the laws of mechanics to molecules we encounter initially two problems. First, there is the question of whether the classical laws of motion which apply to ordinary-sized bodies apply also to molecules. Second, there is the problem of how to deal with the motions of the enormous number of molecules in the smallest quantity of matter which can be subjected to experiment.

It is now known that the answer to the first of these questions is that classical mechanics cannot be applied unchanged to molecules but must be replaced, when necessary, by the laws of quantum mechanics. Fortunately, it turns out that in many problems the calculation, using a slightly modified form of classical mechanics, gives the same result as the more rigorous quantum-mechanical calculation. In broad terms, while solids and the internal structure of molecules must be treated by quantum mechanics the interaction of molecules with each other in fluids can still be treated classically. Only in the case of very light molecules at low temperatures does quantum theory make predictions which differ from the classical theory. In practice there are only three such liquids, liquid helium, liquid hydrogen and, to some extent, liquid neon which show 'quantum behaviour' and about these we shall have little to say.

In one gram molecule of matter there are 6.06×10^{23} molecules, all in motion, and all exerting forces on each other. It is immediately obvious that it is a hopeless task to attempt to follow this motion in detail. Even supposing we could solve the equations of motion, the solutions would tell us nothing about the thermodynamic properties of the fluid. Any measurement we make on matter in bulk will yield a result which depends on some averaged property of the molecules. The science which gives information about the behaviour of large numbers is the science of statistics and so we must combine our laws of mechanics with a proper statistical treatment. In this way we arrive at a science of Statistical Mechanics as the connecting link between the properties of matter in bulk and the mechanics of the individual molecules.

Before outlining these methods in more detail we shall derive an important relation between the intermolecular force law for a simple fluid and the equation of state, which illustrates this averaging process. This relation is due to Clausius and is known as the Virial Theorem.

Clausius' Virial Theorem

Let us consider a vessel in the form of a cube of side l with the origin of a cartesian coordinate system at the centre, the axes being perpendicular to the faces. Let the box contain a large number N of fluid molecules, regarded as small spherical particles. As the molecules move about each will be subject to a rapidly fluctuating force. Suppose that at some instant the force on a molecule i at the point x_i, y_i, z_i, is resolved into its cartesian components X_i, Y_i, Z_i. Then, if m is the mass of a molecule, Newton's second law is, for the motion in the x-direction,

$$X_i = m \frac{d^2 x_i}{dt^2} \quad \text{or} \quad X_i x_i = m x_i \frac{d^2 x_i}{dt^2} \qquad 5.15$$

We write the right-hand side of the second equation of 5.15 in terms of the velocities and the coordinates. This we may do by noting that

$$\frac{m}{2} \frac{d}{dt} \left(\frac{dx_i^2}{dt} \right) = m \frac{d}{dt} \left(x_i \cdot \frac{dx_i}{dt} \right) = m x_i \cdot \frac{d^2 x_i}{dt^2} + m \left(\frac{dx_i}{dt} \right)^2 \qquad 5.16$$

Eliminating the acceleration term, $m x_i (d^2 x_i / dt^2)$, and putting u_i equal to the x-component of velocity, dx_i/dt, we obtain

$$\frac{m}{2} \frac{d}{dt} \left(\frac{dx_i^2}{dt} \right) = X_i x_i + m u_i^2 \qquad 5.17$$

with similar equations for the y and z components. Adding the three equations so obtained we get

$$\frac{m}{2} \frac{d}{dt} \left\{ \frac{d}{dt} (x_i^2 + y_i^2 + z_i^2) \right\} = X_i x_i + Y_i y_i + Z_i z_i + m c_i^2 \qquad 5.18$$

where $c_i^2 = u_i^2 + v_i^2 + w_i^2$, v_i and w_i being the y and z components of velocity and c_i the resultant velocity. The quantity $x_i^2 + y_i^2 + z_i^2 = r_i^2$ is the square of the distance of the molecule from the centre of the box, r_i. As time goes on this distance will vary, but it cannot increase without limit, since the molecule must remain in the box. If we write down similar equations for all the N molecules and add them, the terms on the left will, over a long time, average to zero, for the fluid as a whole is neither expanding nor contracting. Denoting the summation by the sign $\sum$ we obtain

$$\sum_i (X_i x_i + Y_i y_i + Z_i z_i) = -\sum_i m c_i^2 = -2U_{kin} \qquad 5.19$$

where U_{kin} is the kinetic energy of the fluid, $\sum_i \frac{1}{2} m c_i^2$. We shall see later that for monatomic fluids U_{kin} has the same value as for an ideal monatomic gas, namely, $\frac{3}{2}NkT$. The summation term involving the forces and coordinates is known as the Virial of Clausius.

Let us now examine more closely the force acting on a fluid molecule. It will be made up from two contributions. First, there will be the force due to all the other fluid molecules. Secondly, there will be the forces due to the molecules of the solid which make up the walls of the box. We may then split the component X_i into two parts, $X_i = X_i' + X_i''$ where X_i' is the force due to the fluid molecules and X_i'' the wall force, giving two virial terms in 5.19. The average value of the virial of the wall forces can, however, be simply related to the pressure. X_i'' will only have a significant magnitude when the molecule comes close to the wall—within a few Ångstrom units. Let us consider a small area, δA, of the wall of the box at $x = l/2$. By Newton's third law the force exerted on a fluid molecule by the wall is equal and opposite to the force exerted by the fluid molecule on the wall. If we consider the summation $\sum_i X_i'' x_i$ for those molecules which come close to δA, we may replace the coordinate of the molecules, x_i, by the coordinate of the wall, $l/2$, with negligible error, and the x-component of the sum of the forces X_i'' by the negative of the force on the wall. But this is just $-p\,\delta A$ and is along the x-direction, showing that the y and z contributions to the summation average to zero. For this part of the virial we get, then, $-p\,\delta A \cdot l/2$ and for the whole face, of area l^2, we get $-pl^3/2 = -pV/2$. The face at $x = -l/2$ contributes an equal amount (the sign of the coordinate and the direction of the pressure both being reversed), giving $-pV$. The other pairs of faces give equal contributions, so the virial of the wall-forces reduces to $-3pV$. The virial equation now becomes

$$\sum_i (X_i' x_i + Y_i' y_i + Z_i' z_i) - 3pV = -3NkT \qquad 5.20$$

where we now need to consider only the forces due to the fluid molecules, X_i', etc.

As both X_i' and x_i, etc., can be positive or negative with equal probability, it might at first sight appear that when we sum over all the molecules the first term will average to zero. This is not so, however, because the forces on neighbouring molecules are not statistically independent, as may be seen as follows. Consider† a pair of molecules, i and j, separated by a distance r_{ij}. Let X_{ij}' be the part of

† A generalised Virial Theorem is discussed in ch. 9 and the reader may find it helpful to refer to fig. 9.2, p. 144. In fig. 9.2 $(x_i - x_j)$ is denoted by x_{ij}.

X' due to molecule j, and similarly X'_{ji} that part of the force on j due to molecule i. Then, again by Newton's third law, $X'_{ij} = -X'_{ji}$. The contribution of these terms to the virial is

$$x_i X'_{ij} + x_j X'_{ji} = X'_{ij}(x_i - x_j) \qquad 5.21$$

For central forces the force between i and j is directed along r_{ij}. If its magnitude is $F(r_{ij})$, the component along the x-direction, X'_{ij} is $F(r_{ij})\{(x_i - x_j)/r_{ij}\}$, since $(x_i - x_j)/r_{ij}$ is the cosine of the angle between r_{ij} and the x-direction. Thus the above contribution to the virial is $F(r_{ij})(x_i - x_j)^2/r_{ij}$. Adding the y and z contributions gives

$$\frac{F(r_{ij})}{r_{ij}} \{(x_i - x_j)^2 + (y_i - y_j)^2 + (z_i - z_j)^2\} = r_{ij} F(r_{ij})$$

Summing over all pairs of molecules we get $\sum_{\text{pairs}} r_{ij} \cdot F(r_{ij})$ which does not, in general, vanish.

Putting this summation in eq. 5.20 we arrive at the final equation,

$$pV = NkT + \frac{1}{3} \overline{\sum_{\text{pairs}} r_{ij} \cdot F(r_{ij})} \qquad 5.22$$

which is the form of the Virial Theorem for molecules with central additive forces. We have derived it for the special shape of a cubic container; it can be shown to be true for any shape of container. The bar over the summation is to indicate that this term is the result of averaging processes involving both the time and the coordinates of the molecules. We have not been very precise about the nature of these averaging processes and we now turn to a closer examination of how averages of molecular properties are to be obtained in general.

The method we use is due to Gibbs. The system of N molecules occupies a volume V at a fixed temperature T and is imagined to be in thermal equilibrium with its surroundings. As exchange of energy with these surroundings is allowed, the internal energy and all other thermodynamic properties are not absolutely constant but fluctuate in time about mean values. The fluctuations are, however, so minute when N is large as to be far beyond experimental detection and so only the mean value is of interest. Gibbs' method then gives directly the free energy F, or, strictly, its mean value, in terms of N, V and T.

In Gibbs' method we begin as though we were to attempt a detailed calculation of the motion of all the molecules. That is, we erect coordinate systems which allow us to specify (in imagination) the positions and momenta of the N molecules at some instant of time. We then observe that certain distributions of the molecules in space and momentum are more probable than others and, by using the laws of probability, these distributions can be found. The molecular motion in a system in equilibrium can be regarded as continuously changing the distribution, so that during the period of a measurement all possible distributions may be generated. The measured value of any property which is a function of the coordinates and momenta will then be a properly weighted mean value averaged over the time.

Gibbs preferred a somewhat different interpretation; he imagined a very large number of identical copies of the actual system all with the same values of N, V, T, but differing at any instant of time in their molecular distributions. These hypothetical copies constitute, in Gibbs' terminology, a canonical ensemble (assembly) of systems, and the averaging process is applied at any instant to this ensemble. For equilibrium properties either interpretation is allowable but for non-equilibrium properties, which we shall encounter in chs. 9 and 10, there are reasons for distinguishing between 'ensemble averaging' and 'time averaging'.

Probability

In the application of statistical methods to physical problems there are three simple theorems in probability theory which are useful. The first of these is the Multiplication Theorem, which is as follows: 'If the probability of success in one trial is P_1 and that in another is P_2 and these probabilities are independent, then the probability, P, that both successes occur is $P = P_1 \times P_2$.'

Thus the probability, P_1, of drawing an ace of spades from a pack of cards is $\frac{1}{52}$. The probability of obtaining a head when a coin is tossed, P_2, is $\frac{1}{2}$. The outcome of the card experiment in no way affects the fall of the coin, so the probabilities are independent. The probability that an ace and a head are obtained is then $\frac{1}{52} \times \frac{1}{2} = \frac{1}{104}$. The result is easily generalised to a number of independent trials, $1, 2, \ldots, N$, that is, $P = P_1 \times P_2 \times P_3, \ldots, P_N$.

A related theorem is, 'If the probability of an outcome, a, in a trial is P_1 and if, after a success has occurred the probability of an outcome, b, is P_2, then the probability that a is followed by b is again $P = P_1 \times P_2$.' Thus the probability of drawing the ace of spades, retaining it, and then drawing the ace of clubs is $P = \frac{1}{52} \times \frac{1}{51}$, for after the first ace is drawn the number of cards is reduced by one. The probabilities are not independent in the sense that the conditions of the second trial have been altered by the outcome of the first, but thereafter the selection of the second card is unaffected.

The third theorem is the Addition Theorem. 'If the probabilities of a number of alternative and mutually exclusive outcomes of a trial are P_1, P_2, P_3, etc., then the probability, P, that one or another of these will occur in a single trial is $P = P_1 + P_2 + P_3 + \cdots$.' Thus the probability, P, of drawing a spade from a pack is the sum of the probabilities of drawing the ace of spades, the two of spades, the three of spades, etc. Each outcome excludes the others and each has a probability $\frac{1}{52}$. The required result is then $P = \frac{1}{52} + \frac{1}{52} + \cdots = \frac{13}{52} = \frac{1}{4}$. If all possible outcomes are included the sum must be unity, corresponding to absolute certainty that one must occur. The probabilities are then said to be mutually exclusive and exhaustive.

Continuous probability

Suppose we seek information about the variation of height of adult males in a country. We cannot ask: 'What is the probability that a man selected at random is exactly 6 ft tall?' for, if we suppose our measuring apparatus is of unlimited precision, no man would be found to be of *exactly* this height. Instead we may ask: 'What is the probability that a man has a height, z, between 6·00 ft and 6·01 ft?' In this form the question is meaningful, to answer it we could (in principle) measure all the men in the country, say n in number, and find the number, δn, in the above range. The required probability is the ratio of δn to n. In general for a quantity z which can vary continuously, like height, we may ask: 'What is the probability of a value between z and $z + \delta z$?' If the interval of height δz is not too large the number, δn, of men in it will be, among other factors, proportional to its size. We may then say

$$\frac{\delta n}{n} = f(z)\,\delta z \qquad\qquad 5.23$$

where $f(z)$ depends on the multitude of biological factors which control height in men. For very large or very small z, $f(z)$ will be small, indicating the rarity of giants or dwarfs in the population and will have a larger value in the vicinity of the average height.

$f(z)$ is called a probability distribution function. It is not itself a probability but becomes one when multiplied by δz.

If we apply our Addition Theorem to all possible intervals we must find for the probability that a selected man has a height between zero and infinity, the result unity. This follows at once for

$$\sum f(z) . \delta z = \frac{\sum \delta n}{n} = \frac{n}{n} = 1 \qquad\qquad 5.24$$

In the limit when δz is very small this becomes

$$\int_0^\infty f(z) \, \mathrm{d}z = 1 \qquad\qquad 5.25$$

Joint probability distributions
Suppose a marksman fires a large number of shots at a point, 0, in a target, fig. 5.2. If we take Cartesian coordinates, x and y, with

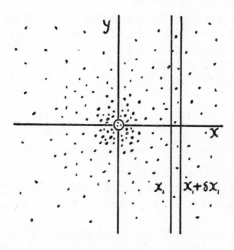

Fig. 5.2   Distribution of shots fired at a point, 0, of a target

centre 0, we may ask: 'What is the probability that a shot lands in a region lying between x and $x + \delta x$ and y and $y + \delta y$?' This region is a small rectangle of area $\delta x . \delta y$ and the probability of hitting it will be proportional, among other factors, to this area. It will also depend on how far the region is from 0, that is, on x and y. We may denote the probability by

$$\frac{\delta n(x, y)}{n} = f(x, y) \, \delta x . \delta y \qquad 5.26$$

where $\delta n(x, y)/n$ is the fraction of the total number of shots in $\delta x . \delta y$. The function $f(x, y)$ will have small values if x, or y, or both, are large and its study will tell us something about the skill of the marksman. Such a function is called a joint probability distribution function.

Since a shot must land somewhere we must require

$$\int_{x=-\infty}^{x=+\infty} \int_{y=-\infty}^{y=+\infty} f(x, y) \, \mathrm{d}x \, \mathrm{d}y = 1 \qquad 5.27$$

The extension of this process to any number of variables is obvious.

Reduced probability distribution

If we enquire only about the distribution of shots in the x-direction, that is, in the probability that a shot lands somewhere in the fixed vertical strip between x_1 and $x_1 + \delta x_1$, then we may fix the variable x at this value x_1. The Addition Theorem, applied to the variable y only, then tells us that, if the required probability be denoted by $g(x_1) \, \mathrm{d}x_1$

$$g(x_1) \, \mathrm{d}x_1 = \int_{y=-\infty}^{y=+\infty} f(x_1, y) \, \mathrm{d}x_1 \, \mathrm{d}y = \mathrm{d}x_1 \int_{y=-\infty}^{y=+\infty} f(x_1, y) \, \mathrm{d}y \qquad 5.28$$

When the integration has been carried out and the limits put in, the variable y disappears, leaving $g(x_1)$, a function of x_1 only. A function like $g(x_1)$ obtained in this way is called a reduced distribution function.

Again these results may be generalised to any number of variables. For N variables $x, y, z, \ldots$ a joint distribution will have the form

$$f(x, y, z, \ldots) \, \mathrm{d}x \, \mathrm{d}y \, \mathrm{d}z \ldots \qquad 5.29$$

and must satisfy the condition that when N integrations are performed over the complete ranges of each variable the result must be unity. By integrating over a lesser number of variables, reduced distribution functions are obtained for the remaining variables.

The calculation of average values

Let us return to our distribution function for the heights of adult males and see how we may use it to calculate average values. Suppose, for example, we wish to know the average height of the male population. This could be obtained by adding the heights of every man in the population and dividing by the total number of men. In terms of our distribution function the result is obtained as follows. The number of men in the interval between z and $z + \delta z$ is δn. These men will contribute a quantity $z \cdot \delta n$ to the above sum. The total sum is then $\sum z \cdot \delta n$ and the average $\sum z \, \delta n / n$. But $\delta n / n$ is just $f(z) \cdot \delta z$ and in the limit when the sum becomes an integral we obtain for the average height, $\bar{z}$,

$$\bar{z} = \int_0^\infty z \cdot f(z) \, dz \qquad 5.30$$

Here the bar denotes an average value. In words this formula reads: 'To find the average value multiply the quantity to be averaged by the distribution function and integrate over the entire range of the variable.'

This result is again easily generalised to joint distribution functions. If we have any quantity which depends on variables $x, y, z, \ldots$ say some function $G(x, y, z, \ldots)$ then the average value, $\bar{G}$, is obtained from the formula

$$\bar{G} = \int \ldots \int G(x, y, z, \ldots) f(x, y, z, \ldots) \, dx \, dy \, dz \ldots \qquad 5.31$$

where the integrations extend over all the ranges of all the variables.

Distribution functions for fluids

Suppose a large number, N, of molecules are confined to a fixed volume V. We shall ignore the complexities of molecular structure and regard them as small spherical particles which have, however, been labelled $i, j, k, \ldots$ in some way so that one molecule may be distinguished from another. To locate the positions of these molecules we may, with the aid of a Cartesian coordinate system, divide up the volume V into small volume elements $\delta x \, \delta y \, \delta z$. If we select one element, say $\delta V_1 = \delta x_1 \, \delta y_1 \, \delta z_1$ the probability that a particular molecule, say that labelled i, has at some instant, its centre within this element will be proportional to the volume, δV_1.

If we now consider a joint probability distribution for all the N

molecules, that is, the probability at some instant that molecule i is in δV_1, molecule j in δV_2 and so on for all the molecules, then this joint probability will be, among other factors, proportional to the product $\delta V_1 \delta V_2 \ldots \delta V_N$. For economy in writing we denote this product of N volume elements (or $3N$ coordinate elements) by $\delta \mathscr{V}_N$.

In a very similar way we can specify the resultant momentum p_i of molecule i by Cartesian components p_{xi}, p_{yi}, p_{zi}. We may then use the natural and helpful analogy of a 'momentum space' divided into 'volume' elements $\delta p_1, \delta p_2, \ldots, \delta p_N$ to infer that the joint probability that molecule i has a resultant momentum in the element δp_1, molecule j in δp_2 and so on is proportional to $\delta p_1 \delta p_2 \delta p_i \ldots \delta p_N$, and this product we abbreviate to $\delta \mathscr{P}_N$.

Finally, by combining both space and momentum distributions, we conclude that the overall joint probability that both specifications are met is, among other factors, proportional to, $\delta V_1 \delta V_2 \ldots \delta V_N$ $\delta p_1 \delta p_2 \ldots \delta p_N$ or, in short, to $\delta \mathscr{V}_N \delta \mathscr{P}_N$.

We now enquire what are the 'other factors' on which this probability depends. If we take two or more volume elements which are very close to each other in ordinary space, the repulsive forces between molecules will reduce the probability of simultaneous occupation. Again, the likelihood that an appreciable number of molecules can acquire momenta very much greater than the general average (by, say, lucky 'collisions' with their neighbours) is also small. We must expect our joint probability distribution function to become much smaller than normal in such cases.

When two or more molecules are sufficiently close together their mutual potential energy becomes very large and positive. Similarly, if a number of molecules have large momenta their total kinetic energy is large and positive. This leads us to suspect that there is a relation between the magnitude of the total energy of the system and the corresponding probability, the connection being such that, for example, large positive values of part of this energy distributed among a few favoured molecules, with reduced rations for the rest, will correspond to a small value for the joint probability distribution function. We therefore take our joint probability distribution for the N molecules, which we write as $f_{Ns} \delta \mathscr{V}_N \delta \mathscr{P}_N$, as depending in some way on their total energy function, H,

$$f_{Ns} \delta \mathscr{V}_N \delta \mathscr{P}_N = \chi(H) \delta \mathscr{V}_N \delta \mathscr{P}_N \qquad\qquad 5.32$$

The suffix s denotes that distributions of labelled or specified molecules are implied. H is the sum of the kinetic and potential energies of the N molecules expressed in terms of their coordinates and momenta, that is

$$H = \sum_{i=1}^{N} \frac{p_i^2}{2m} + \Phi \qquad 5.33$$

where Φ is the total potential energy, which depends on the coordinates. Expressed in this way H is called the Hamiltonian form of the energy.

The form of the unknown function, $\chi(H)$, we obtain by the following argument. Consider two containers, one with N molecules and one with M, and denote quantities referring to this second system by dashes on the appropriate symbols. If the containers are separated so that they cannot interact in any way, the two probability distributions are independent. We may then apply the first Multiplication Theorem to set up the joint probability distribution for both systems. This is

$$(f_{Ns}\, \delta \mathscr{V}_N\, \delta \mathscr{P}_N) \times (f'_{Ms}\, \delta \mathscr{V}'_M\, \delta \mathscr{P}'_M) \qquad 5.34$$

so

$$f_{Ns} . f'_{Ms}\, \delta \mathscr{V}_N\, \delta \mathscr{V}'_M\, \delta \mathscr{P}_N\, \delta \mathscr{P}'_M = \chi(H) . \chi(H')\, \delta \mathscr{V}_N\, \delta \mathscr{V}'_M\, \delta \mathscr{P}_N\, \delta \mathscr{P}'_M$$

Suppose now the containers are brought into proximity with each other so that the molecules in each can interact weakly with those in the other. Suppose further that the temperatures are equal. Then there will be no net flow of energy from one to the other so the probability distributions will be virtually unchanged. There will be only a slight disturbance depending on a small interaction energy, δH, say. We may nevertheless suppose that this interaction energy δH is sufficient to permit us to regard our containers as forming a combined system (in which, that is, the effect of any future disturbance we might make to one system will eventually, given sufficient time, be communicated to the other). For the combined system we may write down the overall probability distribution which, if it is to be of universal validity, must have the same form as the individual systems, that is, it must be of the form

$$\chi(H + H' + \delta H)\, \delta \mathscr{V}_N\, \delta \mathscr{V}'_M\, \delta \mathscr{P}_N\, \delta \mathscr{P}'_M \qquad 5.35$$

On comparing with 5.34 we see that in the limit, when δH may be neglected in comparison with H and H', we must require

$$\chi(H) . \chi(H') = \chi(H + H') \qquad 5.36$$

This functional equation is satisfied only by one very simple function, the exponential function. Thus, if we take

$$\chi(H) \propto \exp -\beta H$$

we get

$$\exp -\beta H \times \exp -\beta H' = \exp -\beta(H+H') \qquad 5.37$$

where β is a positive constant, the same for each system. The negative sign is required if our probabilities are to remain finite for arbitrarily large values of H.

The argument can be extended to any number of systems containing any kind of molecule, provided only that their temperatures are the same. We have seen that β must then also be the same for all systems and this suggests that β is related in some way to the temperature. If we choose one especially simple system for which β can be calculated we shall know this value applies to all systems, no matter how complex.

A very simple system is a monatomic gas whose behaviour, when sufficiently rarified, can be made to approximate as closely as we please to an ideal gas. Bringing such a system close to any other and observing whether or not there is a flow of energy between them is then seen to be a familiar experimental operation. It is just what we do when we measure temperature with a gas thermometer. We shall see later that for an ideal monatomic gas β can indeed be found and has the value $\beta = 1/kT$, where $k = R/N$ is Boltzmann's Constant. For economy we shall usually continue to use the symbol β in our distribution function which now has the form

$$f_{Ns}.\delta\mathscr{V}_N.\delta\mathscr{P}_N. \propto \exp -\beta H.\delta\mathscr{V}_N.\delta\mathscr{P}_N \qquad 5.38$$

and lacks only a constant of proportionality before we can replace the variation sign by a sign of equality. If we denote this constant by $1/C$ we may use the Addition Theorem to find it. We must require that the sum of all possible distributions be unity, or in the limit when this sum becomes an integral,

$$1 = \frac{1}{C} \int \exp(-\beta H)\, d\mathscr{V}_N.d\mathscr{P}_N \qquad 5.39$$

where the single integral sign really represents repeated integrations over all possible ranges of all the variables, thereby exhausting all possible distributions. Thus

$$C = \int \exp(-\beta H) \, d\mathscr{V}_N \, d\mathscr{P}_N$$

so that

$$f_{Ns} \, d\mathscr{V}_N \, d\mathscr{P}_N = \frac{\exp(-\beta H) . d\mathscr{V}_N . d\mathscr{P}_N}{\int \exp(-\beta H) . d\mathscr{V}_N . d\mathscr{P}_N} \qquad 5.40$$

This is a fundamental formula from which all the thermodynamic properties of any system of molecules obeying classical laws can, in principle, be calculated. The factor $\exp -\beta H$ which appears in it is the 'Boltzmann factor'. In words, the formula states that the probability of finding our physical system in a state of total energy H is proportional to $\exp -\beta H$.

In evaluating the multiple integrals in 5.40 we are assisted by the convenient factorisation property of the exponential function. Thus, using 5.33, the Boltzmann factor may be written

$$\exp -\beta H = \left(\exp -\beta \sum \frac{p_i^2}{2m}\right)(\exp -\beta \Phi)$$

Further, as the kinetic part of the Hamiltonian does not depend on the coordinates and the potential part does not depend on the momenta, we may separate the integration into products of momentum integrals and coordinate (or volume) integrals. The denominator, C, of 5.40 becomes

$$C = \int \exp -\beta \frac{\sum p_i^2}{2m} \, d\mathscr{P}_N \times \int \exp -\beta \Phi \, d\mathscr{V}_N \qquad 5.41$$

where $d\mathscr{P}_N = dp_1, dp_2, \ldots, dp_N$ and $d\mathscr{V}_N = dV_1, dV_2, \ldots, dV_N$. The first integral expression can be easily evaluated. It can again be factored into a product of integrals of the type $\int \exp -\beta(p_{xi}^2/2m) \, dp_{xi}$ where p_{xi} is the x-component of momentum of the ith molecule so that $p_i^2 = p_{xi}^2 + p_{yi}^2 + p_{zi}^2$ and $dp_i = dp_{xi} . dp_{yi} . dp_{zi}$. In all there are $3N$ of these integrals, from the three momentum components of each of the N molecules. Each component may range from $-\infty$ to $+\infty$ so that all the integrals are of the same mathematical form which we may write as $\int_{-\infty}^{+\infty} \exp -\alpha t^2 \, dt$ where $\alpha = \beta/2m$ and t stands for any of the

$3N$ momenta. This is the well-known Gauss error integral and has the value $\sqrt{\pi/\alpha}$. The product of these integrals is then $(\pi/\alpha)^{3N/2}$. Putting $\alpha = \beta/2m = (1/2mkT)$ reduces the integrals over the momenta in 5.41 to $(2\pi mkT)^{3N/2}$. Finally, we have

$$C = (2\pi mkT)^{3N/2} \int \exp -\beta\Phi \, \mathrm{d}\mathscr{V}_N \qquad\qquad 5.42$$

We cannot apply a similar procedure to the other factor in C, because the total potential energy Φ depends on the coordinates of all the molecules in such a complicated way that it cannot be written as the sum of terms each involving the coordinates of one molecule only. In this fact lies the whole difficulty of the equilibrium theory of liquids.

There are three different ways in which we may proceed from here on, all of which take 5.40 as their starting point. These we may call the Method of Averages, the Method of Reduced Distribution Functions and the Partition Function Method.

The method of averages

We may use eq. 5.40 to calculate the average value of any quantity which depends on the molecular coordinates and momenta. One of the most important of these is the internal energy U, that is, the average value of the energy function of the molecules H, which we write $U = \bar{H}$. From the rule given mathematically in 5.31 this average is

$$U = \bar{H} = \int H.f_{NS}.\mathrm{d}\mathscr{V}_N.\mathrm{d}\mathscr{P}_N = \frac{\int H \exp(-\beta H).\mathrm{d}\mathscr{V}_N.\mathrm{d}\mathscr{P}_N}{\int \exp(-\beta H).\mathrm{d}\mathscr{V}_N.\mathrm{d}\mathscr{P}_N}$$

$$5.43$$

This expression will, therefore, give us the caloric equation of state. Similarly, the average of the virial of the intermolecular forces $\overline{\sum_{\text{pairs}} r_{ij}.F(r_{ij})}$ will, from 5.22, give us the ordinary equation of state. The attempts which have been made to evaluate such expressions we shall discuss later.

The method of reduced distribution functions

Again from formula 5.40 we may obtain various kinds of reduced distribution functions. By integrating the numerator over all momenta, for example, we may obtain the distribution function for molecules in space only, the configurational distribution function for N molecules. Or by continuing the process and further integrating over the coordinates of all but a number, h, of molecules we may obtain the probability that h specified molecules occupy fixed volume elements $\delta V_1, \delta V_2, \ldots, \delta V_h$. This will be the reduced configurational distribution for h molecules, and to distinguish configurational distributions we shall use the symbol n_{hs}. Thus

$$n_{hs}\, dV_1 \ldots dV_h = \frac{dV_1 \ldots dV_h \int \exp(-\beta H) dV_{h+1} \ldots dV_N\, d\mathscr{P}_N}{\int \exp(-\beta H) d\mathscr{V}_N\, d\mathscr{P}_N}$$

5.44

In this expression there are integrals over the complete set of momenta in both numerator and denominator. By using the factorisation property we may cancel these out and so obtain

$$n_{hs}\, dV_1 \ldots dV_h = dV_1 \ldots dV_h \cdot \frac{\int \exp(-\beta \Phi) dV_{h+1} \ldots dV_N}{\int \exp(-\beta \Phi) dV_1 \ldots dV_N}$$

5.45

Configurational distributions prove to be of primary importance in the theory of fluids. In particular, the distribution for $h = 2$ is closely related to the radial distribution function, which is obtained from diffraction experiments. However, such experiments, or indeed any other, cannot tell us which molecules occupy which volume elements for, in reality, all molecules of a pure liquid are indistinguishable. We must therefore see how our formulae are modified when the labels on our molecules are removed.

Specific and generic distributions

For labelled molecules a specific distribution in which, for example, molecule i is in volume element δV_1 and molecule j in δV_2 is counted as a different distribution from one in which j is in δV_1 and i in δV_2. We may, however, employ a distribution function which tells us, for example, the probability that δV_1 and δV_2 are occupied by *any* two of the N molecules. Such distributions are called generic distributions and we shall distinguish them by omitting the suffix s on the appropriate symbols.

The probability of a generic distribution of N molecules among N volume elements is very much greater than the probability of a particular specific distribution. In fact if all the (labelled) molecules are permuted among the elements we obtain $N!$ different arrangements all of which would count as a 'success' in reckoning the generic distribution probability. That is

$$f_N = N! f_{Ns} \qquad\qquad 5.46$$

The reduced distribution functions may be similarly treated. Thus the probability that a number, h, of molecules are in volume elements δV_1 to δV_h, without regard to which molecule is in which, that is, the generic configurational distribution n_h, will be larger than any corresponding specific distribution. In fact, n_h will be equal to n_{hs} times the number of ways in which h molecules can be selected from N labelled molecules and put in a particular order. This is the number of permutations of N objects taken h at a time and is $N(N-1)$ $(N-2) \ldots (N-h+1)$, or $N!/(N-h)!$ Thus,

$$n_h = \frac{N!}{(N-h)!} n_{hs} \qquad\qquad 5.47$$

The full expression for the important pair distribution function n_2 is, using 5.47 and 5.45 with $h=2$

$$n_2\, dV_1 . dV_2 = \frac{N!}{(N-2)!}\, dV_1 . dV_2 \frac{\displaystyle\int \exp(-\beta\Phi) dV_3 \ldots dV_N}{\displaystyle\int \exp(-\beta\Phi) dV_1 \ldots dV_N}$$

$$5.48$$

To check this formula, and illustrate its meaning, let us apply it to an ideal monatomic gas. For ideal gases there is no molecular potential energy, so $\Phi = 0$ for all configurations and $\exp(-\beta\Phi) = 1$. In the denominator of 5.48 there are then simply N repeated integrations over the volume elements each of which yield V, the volume of the system, giving V^N. In the numerator there are $(N-2)$ such integrals, giving V^{N-2}. Thus, finally

$$n_2\, dV_1 . dV_2 = \frac{N!}{(N-2)!}\, dV_1 . dV_2 \frac{V^{N-2}}{V^N} = N(N-1) \frac{dV_1}{V} . \frac{dV_2}{V}$$

$$5.49$$

This result can be obtained directly from first principles by applying our second multiplication theorem to find the probability that any one of the N molecules is in dV_1, which is clearly $N(dV_1/V)$, followed by the probability that, with one molecule so located, any one of the remaining $(N-1)$ will be found in dV_2, which is $(N-1)\,dV_2/V$. The absence of intermolecular forces in an ideal gas means that these probabilities are indeed independent. When N is very large we may neglect unity in comparison with it and in this case therefore

$$n_2 = \left(\frac{N}{V}\right)^2 = \rho_0^2 \quad \text{(ideal gas)} \qquad 5.50$$

In the case of a real fluid the relation of n_2 to the radial distribution function is obtained as follows. As ρ_0 is the number–density of molecules the probability that any volume element, dV_1, chosen at random in a uniform fluid, contains a molecule is $\rho_0\,dV_1$. Now select a second element, dV_2, at a distance r from the first. The probability that this element is occupied when dV_1 is also occupied is not simply $\rho_0\,dV_2$ because the presence of the first molecule alters the number–density near to it. In fact, by definition, the number–density at dV_2 is now $\rho(r)$, so the probability that it is occupied is $\rho(r)dV_2$. The probability that both elements are simultaneously occupied by any two of the N molecules is therefore, by our second multiplication theorem, $\rho_0\,dV_1.\rho(r)dV_2$. But this is just the definition of the quantity $n_2\,dV_1.dV_2$. Hence

$$n_2 = \rho_0.\rho(r) \qquad 5.51$$

At large values of r, $\rho(r)$ approaches† ρ_0 and we recover the same expression as for the ideal gas.

As we shall see in ch. 8 the radial distribution function will also give us the complete thermodynamic properties and, in addition, we can check our calculations relating to it against the diffraction data. The calculation of n_2 from eq. 5.48 is therefore the key problem in this second method.

In conclusion we may remark that a distribution obtained by integrating 5.40 over all coordinates and over all but one of the $3N$

---

† Strictly, at large distances, the probability that dV_2 is occupied is not $\rho_0\,dV_2$, i.e. $(N/V)\,dV_2$, since the fact that dV_1 is known to be occupied leaves only $N-1$ molecules with a chance of being found in dV_2. As before, we may safely neglect unity when N is of the order of Avogadro's Number.

momenta—say all but p_{xi}—gives the celebrated Maxwell Distribution of Velocities (or Momenta). To derive it, one takes the term $\exp-(\beta p_{xi}^2/2m)\ dp_{xi}$ from the Boltzmann factor outside the integrations in the numerator. Cancellation of all the integrals in the numerator with all but one in the denominator, gives the result that the probability that the x-component of momentum of molecule i lies between p_{xi} and $p_{xi}+dp_{xi}$ is $(2\pi mkT)^{-\frac{1}{2}}\exp-(p_{xi}^2/2mkT)dp_{xi}$, which is the Maxwell Distribution. Though it finds its most extensive application in the kinetic theory of gases, this distribution applies equally to classical liquids and solids.

The partition function method

The third method of calculating the thermodynamic properties is perhaps the most simple and elegant of all. It gives us directly the free energy F, from which all the thermodynamic properties follow. It again derives from eq. 5.40, for it can be shown[3] that the free energy is simply related to the denominator of this expression. The relation is

$$F = -kT \ln\left(\frac{1}{h^{3N}N!}\int \exp\left(-\beta H\right)\ d\mathcal{V}_N\ d\mathcal{P}_N\right) = -kT \ln Z$$

$$5.52$$

where

$$Z = \frac{1}{h^{3N}N!}\int \exp\frac{-H}{kT}\ d\mathcal{V}_N\ d\mathcal{P}_N \qquad 5.53$$

The quantity Z is called the partition function and, apart from the extra factor $(1/h^{3N}N!)$, is just the denominator of 5.40. This factor contains h, Planck's constant, which is, of course, characteristic of the quantum theory. The reason for its appearance, and that of $N!$, is as follows. We saw at the outset that the strictly correct laws governing the behaviour of molecules are not classical laws but quantum laws. In quantum theory, moreover, the question of indistinguishability of the particles proves to have subtler implications than those discussed previously. This, strictly, necessitates a revision of our entire statistical procedure. The result of such a revision may, however, be summarised as follows. Except for very light molecules at low temperatures eq. 5.40 may be taken as correct as it stands for the purpose of calculating average values or reduced distribution functions. If we wish to use the partition function method, however, the factor $1/h^{3N}N!$ should be included to conform with quantum requirements. The $N!$ may be regarded as 'correcting' for the indistinguishability of the particles.

To illustrate the use of the partition function we can show that it leads to the same formula for the internal energy as the Method of Averages. The most direct connection between the free and internal energies is the Gibbs–Helmholtz equation,

$$U = F - T\left(\frac{\partial F}{\partial T}\right)_V \qquad 5.12$$

With $F = -kT \ln Z$ we get

$$U = -kT \ln Z + T \frac{\partial}{\partial T}(kT \ln Z)$$

$$= -kT \ln Z + kT\left\{\ln Z + \frac{T}{Z}\left(\frac{\partial Z}{\partial T}\right)_V\right\}$$

$$= \frac{kT^2}{Z}\left(\frac{\partial Z}{\partial T}\right)_V \qquad 5.54$$

To find $(\partial Z/\partial T)_V$ we may differentiate eq. 5.53 under the integral sign, for H and the variables of integration do not depend on T. This gives

$$\left(\frac{\partial Z}{\partial T}\right)_V = \frac{1}{h^{3N}N!}\int\left(\exp\frac{-H}{kT}\right)\cdot\frac{H}{kT^2}\cdot\mathrm{d}\mathscr{V}_N\cdot\mathrm{d}\mathscr{P}_N$$

Putting this in 5.54 and using 5.53 again we get

$$U = \frac{\int H \exp(-H/kT)\,\mathrm{d}\mathscr{V}_N\cdot\mathrm{d}\mathscr{P}_N}{\int \exp(-H/kT)\cdot\mathrm{d}\mathscr{V}_N\cdot\mathrm{d}\mathscr{P}_N}$$

which is eq. 5.43. It will be seen that Planck's constant has cancelled out in the final stage, and this disappearance of h always happens when the partition function is used to find experimentally measurable properties of classical fluids.

6

THE PARTITION FUNCTION METHOD

To obtain the partition function Z for a real fluid we again first integrate eq. 5.53 over the momenta, which gives immediately

$$Z = \left(\frac{2\pi mkT}{h^2}\right)^{3N/2} \frac{1}{N!} \int \exp\left(\frac{-\Phi}{kT}\right) \cdot \mathrm{d}\mathscr{V}_N \qquad 6.1$$

The free energy $F = -kT \ln Z$ can then be written as the sum of two parts:

$$F = F_P(N) + F_Q(N) \qquad 6.2$$

where

$$F_P(N) = -\frac{3NkT}{2} \ln\left(\frac{2\pi mkT}{h^2}\right) \qquad 6.3$$

and

$$F_Q(N) = -kT \ln Q(N) \qquad 6.4$$

with

$$Q(N) = \frac{1}{N!} \int \exp\left(\frac{-\Phi}{kT}\right) \cdot \mathrm{d}\mathscr{V}_N \qquad 6.5$$

The two parts of the free energy $F_P(N)$ and $F_Q(N)$ are derived from the momenta and coordinates respectively. $F_P(N)$ depends only on temperature but not on volume and its complete evaluation means that we may now temporarily lose interest in it and concentrate on $F_Q(N)$, which depends, in general, on both temperature and volume. $F_Q(N)$ is the configurational free energy and properties derived from it, by appropriate differentiations, are configurational properties. We may note that the equation of state, obtained from $p = -(\partial F/\partial V)_T$, is a configurational property, because when 6.2 is differentiated with respect to volume the first term on the right vanishes. Hence,

$$p = -\left(\frac{\partial F_Q(N)}{\partial V}\right)_T \qquad 6.6$$

For an ideal gas $Q(N)$ can be readily evaluated because, as before, $\Phi = 0$ and $\exp(-\beta\Phi) = 1$. The integral in 6.5 becomes, on replacing $d\mathscr{V}_N$ by $dV_1 \dots dV_N$, simply N repeated integrations over the volume which again yields V^N. The *configuration integral*, $Q(N)$, then becomes $V^N/N!$ and we obtain

$$F_Q(N) = -kT\ln\frac{V^N}{N!} \quad \text{(ideal gas)} \qquad 6.7$$

The equation of state is then

$$p = -\left(\frac{\partial F_Q(N)}{\partial V}\right)_T = kT\frac{N!}{V^N}\frac{\partial}{\partial V}\left(\frac{V^N}{N!}\right) = kTN\frac{V^{N-1}}{V^N} \qquad 6.8$$

or $p = NkT/V$, the ideal gas equation of state. The complete partition function is

$$Z = \left(\frac{2\pi mkT}{h^2}\right)^{3N/2}\frac{V^N}{N!} \qquad 6.9$$

The internal energy U is, from eq. 5.54

$$U = \frac{kT^2}{Z}\left(\frac{\partial Z}{\partial T}\right)_V \qquad 6.10$$

For constant volume, Z takes the form, const. $T^{3N/2}$, which gives at once $U = \frac{3}{2}NkT$, the ideal gas caloric equation of state.

All the other thermodynamic properties may be derived from the relation $F = -kT\ln Z$ by the procedures given on p. 71. The expressions given above for p and U help to confirm, incidentally, our identification of β with $1/kT$, for these expressions may be obtained, quite independently, from the kinetic theory of ideal gases.

Real fluids

For real substances the part of the free energy, $F_P(N)$, which derives from the translational kinetic energy of the molecules, has the same value as for the ideal gas and so U_{kin}, which is obtained from $F_P(N)$, has the value $\frac{3}{2}NkT$ for all classical monatomic solids, liquids and gases. The potential energy, Φ, on the other hand is a complicated function of the coordinates, which depends on the particular inter-molecular law of force and so, in general, the direct evaluation of $Q(N)$ and $F_Q(N)$ is impossible. We may, however, make much progress if we restrict the discussion to simple fluids with spherical or nearly spherical molecules. Specifically, we assume from now on:

(a) The total potential energy, Φ, can be written $\Phi = \sum_{\text{pairs}} \phi(r_{ij})$ (the assumption of additivity, p. 63).

(b) The intermolecular potential function $\phi(r_{ij})$ depends only on the distance r_{ij} between the centres of molecules i and j and can be written in the form $\phi(r_{ij}) = \epsilon f(r_{ij}/\sigma)$, that is, it has the same form for all fluids and depends on only two constants, ϵ and σ, characteristic of particular fluid.

The types of fluid we have in mind are the heavier inert gases and particularly argon, whose properties have been investigated experimentally most extensively and carefully. Typical examples of $\phi(r_{ij})$ are the functions of ch. 4 (p. 62, 63) and, especially, the Lennard–Jones 6–12 function.

Imperfect gases—the cluster expansion method of Mayer

The two assumptions (a) and (b) do not, of themselves, make the evaluation of the configuration integral $Q(N)$ any easier, except in the case of a slightly imperfect gas. In such a gas one molecule will only rarely come near another, and this permits an approximate evaluation of $Q(N)$. The assumption of additivity enables us to write $\exp(-\beta\Phi)$ as a product of factors for each pair of molecules, of which a typical one is $\exp-\beta\phi(r_{ij})$. When molecules i and j are far apart $\phi(r_{ij})$ is nearly zero and $\exp-\beta\phi(r_{ij})$ is nearly unity. If then we introduce a new function $\lambda_{ij} = (\exp-\beta\phi(r_{ij}) - 1)$ we have an expression which is practically zero unless two or more molecules are close together. On replacing $\exp-\beta\phi(r_{ij})$ by $(1 + \lambda_{ij})$ for each pair of molecules in the configuration integral, we find we can write a series of terms involving integrals over products of the λ_{ij} for the different pairs. The classification of these integrals requires a lengthy analysis but one which leads eventually to the coefficients of the virial form of the equation of state, written in inverse powers of the volume. This procedure was developed by Mayer and is known as the *cluster expansion* method, since the successive terms in the virial can be related to groups or clusters of two, three, four, etc., molecules. The expression obtained for the second virial coefficient, for example, is

$$B = -2\pi N \int_0^\infty [\exp(-\beta\phi(r)) - 1]r^2 \, dr \qquad 6.11$$

The integral is readily evaluated for simple forms of $\phi(r)$. For ideal gases $\phi(r) = 0$ and $B = 0$. For hard spheres of diameter σ, $\phi(r) = \infty$ for $r < \sigma$, and $\phi(r) = 0$ for $r > \sigma$, which leads immediately to the result that B is four times the total volume of the spheres. (This is then the quantity b which appears in van der Waals' equation of state, as may be seen from the virial expansion of that equation (2.15), when the term a/RTV, due to the attractive forces, is omitted.) For the Lennard–Jones potential function the evaluation of B is a little more complex but gives the correct form of the dependence of B on temperature. As previously indicated (p. 21) one may then determine ϵ and σ by finding the values which give the best fit to the experimental data.

The expressions for the higher virial coefficients $C, D, \ldots$ become increasingly complex. Virial coefficients up to the fifth have been evaluated for hard spheres and lower coefficients for other simple intermolecular potential functions, and Mayer's method also throws much light on the difficult problem of condensation. At liquid densities, however, the assumptions of the cluster expansion method are clearly invalid and the virial expansion fails to converge, so we shall not pursue this method further.

The Law of Corresponding States

Still without actually evaluating $Q(N)$ we can, with our assumptions (a) and (b), deduce the Law of Corresponding States by an argument based on dimensional analysis, as follows.

Any spatial configuration of molecules in a fluid will have a certain potential energy. If we measure distances in this configuration in terms of the characteristic length σ appropriate to the fluid and energies in terms of the characteristic energy ϵ, we can write our configurational properties in terms of these two constants and Boltzmann's constant k. From the theory of dimensions we find for the dimensions of pressure, volume per molecule, and temperature

$$[p] = \frac{[\text{Energy}]}{[\text{Length}]^3}; \qquad \left[\frac{V}{N}\right] = [\text{Length}]^3; \qquad [T] = \frac{[\text{Energy}]}{[k]}$$

If we therefore put

$$\left(\frac{r_{ij}}{\sigma}\right) = r_{ij}^*; \qquad p = \frac{\epsilon}{\sigma^3} p^*; \qquad \left(\frac{V}{N}\right) = \sigma^3 V^*; \qquad T = \frac{\epsilon}{k} T^*$$

$$6.12$$

the quantities r_{ij}^*, p^*, V^* and T^* are pure numbers which are called *reduced properties in molecular units*. We can now show that p^* must be the same function of V^* and T^* for all substances.

The pressure is derived from $Q(N)$ by eqs. 6.4 and 6.6 which together give

$$p = \frac{kT}{Q(N)} \left(\frac{\partial Q(N)}{\partial V}\right)_T \qquad 6.13$$

Substituting for p, V, and T in this equation the expressions for these quantities in terms of the reduced units this becomes

$$p^* = \frac{T^*}{N} \frac{1}{Q(N)} \left(\frac{\partial Q(N)}{\partial V^*}\right)_{T^*} \qquad 6.14$$

To express $Q(N)$ in reduced measures we note that, with our assumptions (a) and (b),

$$\Phi = \sum_{\text{pairs}} \phi(r_{ij}) = \sum_{\text{pairs}} f\left(\frac{r_{ij}}{\sigma}\right) = \epsilon \sum_{\text{pairs}} f(r_{ij}^*) \qquad 6.15$$

so that

$$\exp\left(-\Phi/kT\right) = \exp\left[-\sum_{\text{pairs}} f(r_{ij}^*)/T^*\right] \qquad 6.16$$

Furthermore, as the volumes of similar figures are proportional to the cubes of their linear dimensions we may put for the volume elements $dV_1 = \sigma^3 dV_1^*$, etc. We thus obtain

$$Q(N) = \frac{\sigma^{3N}}{N!} \int \exp\left[-\sum_{\text{pairs}} f(r_{ij}^*)/T^*\right] dV_1^* \ldots dV_N^* \qquad 6.17$$

When this expression is put in 6.14 the σ^{3N} cancels, so that the right-hand side of 6.14 depends only on reduced quantities but not on ϵ or σ. If we could evaluate the integrals in $Q(N)$ we should obtain a function on the right-hand side of 6.14 which would, therefore, also depend only on V^* and T^*, say $J(V^*, T^*)$. Hence we may write

$$p^* = J(V^*, T^*) \qquad 6.18$$

This is the law of corresponding states, in a slightly different and more general form than that given in ch. 3. To show its relation to the usual form let us imagine that p^*, V^* and T^* are plotted as variables in a Cartesian coordinate system, so that 6.18 represents a surface in this space. Any singular point on this surface, such as the critical point, will have the same molecular reduced coordinates for all substances. Let the reduced coordinates of the critical point be the pure numbers a_1, a_2, a_3, that is, from the equations in 6.12,

$$p_c = \frac{\epsilon}{\sigma^3} a_1; \qquad V_c = N\sigma^3 a_2; \qquad T_c = \frac{\epsilon}{k} a_3 \qquad 6.19$$

For any general point p^*, V^*, T^*, we then have

$$p^* = a_1 \left(\frac{p}{p_c}\right); \qquad V^* = a_2 \left(\frac{V}{V_c}\right); \qquad T^* = a_3 \left(\frac{T}{T_c}\right) \qquad 6.20$$

so that equation 6.18 becomes

$$a_1 \left(\frac{p}{p_c}\right) = J\left(a_2 \left(\frac{V}{V_c}\right); \ a_3 \left(\frac{T}{T_c}\right)\right) \qquad 6.21$$

As a_1, a_2 and a_3 are the same constants for all fluids, this amounts to the statement that p/p_c is a universal function of V/V_c and T/T_c, which is the form of the law given in ch. 3. The values of a_1, a_2 and a_3 can be found when ϵ, σ and the critical constants are known. For spherical molecules and the Lennard–Jones potential function, the best average values derived from experiment are

$$p_c = 0 \cdot 116 \frac{\epsilon}{\sigma^3}; \qquad V_c = 3 \cdot 14 \, N\sigma^3; \qquad T_c = 1 \cdot 25 \frac{\epsilon}{k} \qquad 6.22$$

Conversely, these equations may be used to estimate ϵ and σ for fluids for which only the critical constants have been measured.

Generalising the law of corresponding states we may note that the triple point coordinates in reduced units should also have the same values for all substances, that the reduced saturated vapour pressure should be a universal function of the reduced temperature and so on. All these predictions are very accurately verified for the heavier inert gases, etc. Failure of some solids, liquids and gases to conform to the law, therefore implies that our assumptions (a) and (b) are not valid, or that classical mechanics on which eq. 6.5 depends is not applicable to these substances.

The liquid state

Cell theories of liquids[2]

> . . .and, with assays of bias,
> By indirections, find directions out.   *Hamlet*

The direct evaluation of the partition function for liquids being impossible, it is necessary, to make yet further progress, to adopt a more devious strategy. One group of theories, the cell theories, is based on the attempt to break up the configurational partition function $Q(N)$ into a product of identical similar integrals, one for each molecule, as we did for the momentum integrals. To do this it is necessary to try to express the potential energy of a molecule in a form which will not involve intractable integrations over the coordinates of the $(N-1)$ other molecules.

An intuitive guide to the way this might be possible starts from the idea that in a liquid the local environment of a molecule resembles that in the solid, inasmuch as any molecule is surrounded by near neighbours which restrict its freedom of movement. Each molecule may then tentatively be regarded as confined to a 'cell', the 'walls' of the cell being the nearest neighbours. On this view the chief difference between a solid and a liquid is that, because of the increase in volume in melting, a molecule in a cell has a little more freedom of movement in the liquid than in the solid. This molecule we may therefore call a 'wanderer'. In cell theories it is assumed that the nearest neighbours—the 'wall' molecules—remain fixed in position while the wanderer moves around. Since any molecule may be regarded either as a wall molecule or a wanderer, this involves a paradox, but one which it is necessary to tolerate to make progress.

For a preliminary study of cell theories let us assume that molecules behave as hard non-attracting spheres of diameter σ. In the crystalline solid at $0°K$ these spheres will be in mutual contact in a regular lattice arrangement. The densest possible packings of rigid spheres are the cubic and hexagonal close-packed structures, when each molecule has 12 nearest neighbours. These structures, we recall, are the ones actually found in the solid inert gases.

Fig. 6.1 is a representation, in two dimensions, of the solid and liquid according to this simple cell theory.

In the liquid the lattice is assumed to have expanded uniformly. The disorder in liquids is introduced by supposing that a wanderer W can now bounce freely around in the cell formed by the wall molecules X (in three dimensions there will be twelve wall molecules instead of the six shown). This expansion permits the *centre point* of W to move within the shaded area (volume) called the free volume, V_f. V_f has a complicated shape which is determined by the fact that the centre of W cannot come closer than σ to the centre of a wall molecule. To simplify still further we assume that the free volume can be approximated by a sphere of radius $(a-\sigma)$, that is

$$V_f = \tfrac{4}{3}\pi(a-\sigma)^3 \qquad\qquad 6.23$$

an assumption which slightly underestimates the true free volume.

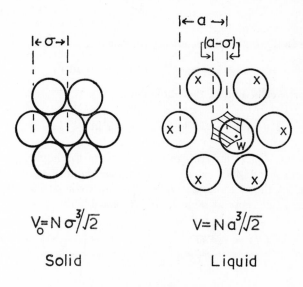

$$V_0 = N\sigma^3/\sqrt{2}$$

$$V = Na^3/\sqrt{2}$$

Solid   Liquid

Fig. 6.1 A two-dimensional representation showing the 'wanderer' molecule (W) and 'wall' molecules (X) in a simple cell model

The basic advantage of the cell method is that, so far as the configurational partition function is concerned, each molecule when permanently confined to its cell may be regarded as an independent thermodynamic system consisting of just one molecule. Therefore, if we work out the configurational free energy for one cell and multiply by the number of cells (equal to the number of molecules N) we should obtain the free energy of the whole liquid.

Our expression for $Q(N)$ is quite general and applies to any number of molecules. On putting $N=1$ and denoting the potential energy of a wanderer by ϕ_1 we get

$$Q(1) = \frac{1}{1!} \int \exp\left(-\phi_1/kT\right) dV_1 \qquad 6.24$$

where $Q(1)$ denotes the configurational partition function for this system of just one molecule. For hard spheres the integral is easily evaluated; $\phi_1=0$ if the centre of W lies within V_f, in which case $\exp\left(-\phi_1/kT\right)=1$, and $\phi_1=\infty$ if the centre is 'outside' V_f (infinite repulsion), in which case $\exp\left(-\phi_1/kT\right)=0$. Hence, in this case, $Q(1)$ is simply equal to V_f.

The configurational free energy for one cell is then

$$F_Q(1) = -kT \ln Q(1) = -kT \ln V_f \qquad 6.25$$

and for N cells, that is, the whole fluid,

$$F_Q(N) = -NkT \ln V_f = -NkT \ln\left\{\frac{4\pi}{3}(a-\sigma)^3\right\} \qquad 6.26$$

To express $F_Q(N)$ in terms of the volume of the liquid we use the geometrical relation between nearest-neighbour distance, a, and volume of the N molecules appropriate to close-packed structures shown in the figure or table 3.1 (p. 36) and obtain

$$F_Q(N) = -NkT \ln \frac{4\pi}{3}\left\{\left(\frac{\sqrt{2}\,V}{N}\right)^{1/3} - \left(\frac{\sqrt{2}\,V_0}{N}\right)^{1/3}\right\}^3 \qquad 6.27$$

or

$$F_Q(N) = -NkT \ln\left(\frac{4\pi\sqrt{2}}{3N}\right) - NkT \ln\left(V^{1/3} - V_0^{1/3}\right)^3 \qquad 6.28$$

Let us calculate the equation of state for our fluid. This is obtained from $p = -[\partial F_Q(N)/\partial V]_T$ which gives, after a little manipulation,

$$\frac{pV}{NkT} = \frac{1}{\{1-(V_0/V)^{1/3}\}} \qquad 6.29$$

where, for one gram molecule, $Nk=R$.

For this equation the pressure goes to infinity when V tends to V_0 (V_0 is the molar volume of the crystal at $0°K$) and to the ideal gas value when V is very large, which is qualitatively the right kind of behaviour. However, for liquids at ordinary pressures it fails hopelessly. For, say, an inert gas at its triple point the experimental value of pV/RT would be approximately unity if V were the molar volume of the *vapour*. As V is actually the molar volume of the *liquid*, pV/RT is very much less than unity. The right-hand side of 6.29 is, on the other hand, much greater than unity because V exceeds V_0 by only about 25%.

The reasons for this failure are not hard to find in view of the many simplifications and approximations we have made, and we now try to improve our model. One of the most serious simplifications is the highly artificial nature of the hard-sphere potential function, and particularly the entire neglect of the effects of the attractive forces. We have supposed that ϕ_1 is zero unless the wanderer touches a neighbour. In fact, the correct choice for the zero of potential energy is for infinite distances between molecules. Now if we bring N molecules together from infinite mutual separations to form a lattice, the system loses potential energy, due to the attractive forces, equal to the lattice potential energy, Φ_L say. When all wanderers are at their cell centres each will have potential energy Φ_L/N, and we may suppose that this will also be approximately the right value for any position of the wanderer in its cell. Our improved potential energy function for one molecule is then

$$\phi_1 = \Phi_L/N \quad \text{(centre within } V_f); \qquad \phi_1 = \infty \quad \text{(centre outside } V_f)$$
$$\text{6.30}$$

and

$$Q(1) = \int \exp\left(-\frac{\phi_1}{kT}\right)dV_1 = \exp\left(-\frac{\Phi_L}{NkT}\right) \cdot V_f \qquad 6.31$$

since the integrand is constant within V_f. Our configurational free energy for N cells is now

$$F_Q(N) = -NkT \ln Q(1) = \Phi_L - NkT \ln V_f \qquad 6.32$$

In this expression Φ_L depends on the lattice spacing and hence on the volume. To estimate it we may perform a lattice energy summation, which procedure leads to the Lennard–Jones and Devonshire type of cell theory (see below). Alternatively we may, at this point, appeal to experiment and put Φ_L equal to the potential internal energy of expansion of the liquid from its actual volume V to infinite volume, $\Phi_L = U_1 - U_\infty$ which we can calculate from experimental data by the methods of ch. 2. From a study of such data Eyring and Hirschfelder[3] conclude that Φ_L for many liquids can be represented quite accurately by a formula, $\Phi_L = -a(T)/V$, where $a(T)$ is a function of temperature only. If we adopt this we obtain

$$F_Q(N) = -NkT \ln V_f - a(T)/V \qquad 6.33$$

which leads to the Eyring Equation of State

$$p = \frac{RT}{V(1-(V_0/V)^{1/3})} - \frac{a(T)}{V^2} \qquad 6.34$$

or

$$\left(p + \frac{a(T)}{V^2}\right)(V - V_0^{1/3} . V^{2/3}) = RT \qquad 6.35$$

This equation is a great improvement on the previous one. It resembles van der Waals' equation and gives a useful semi-empirical description of the properties of liquids.

The theory of Lennard–Jones and Devonshire[4]

Further improvements on the simple theories outlined above leads to the Lennard–Jones and Devonshire theory (abbreviated to L.J.D. in what follows) put forward in 1937. The assumptions of this theory may be summarised as follows.

(1) The basic lattice is chosen as cubic close-packed (f.c.c.).

(2) The potential energy function for a pair of molecules is taken as the L.J. 6–12 function.

(3) The interaction of a wanderer with its twelve neighbours is simplified by supposing that these are distributed with equal probability ('smeared') over the surface of a sphere of radius a_1, thereby giving a spherical cell in which ϕ_1 is a function only of the distance r from the centre; $\phi_1 = \phi_1(r)$.

(4) The potential energy of the system when the molecules are at their cell centres, Φ_L, is calculated by a lattice summation.

As before, we may attribute a potential energy Φ_L/N to each wanderer when all wanderers are at the centres of their cells. When one is at a distance r let its potential energy be $E(r)$ above this value so that

$$\phi_1 = \phi_1(r) = (\Phi_L/N) + E(r) \qquad 6.36$$

The authors first investigated mathematically the variation of $E(r)$ of the wanderer as it moves from the centre to the wall for various values of the ratio (a/σ) with the results shown in fig. 6.2. At high densities the potential rises steeply due to the repulsion of the walls as the wanderer moves from the centre. In more expanded lattices the attractive forces are more evident, for the potential has then a small maximum at the centre.

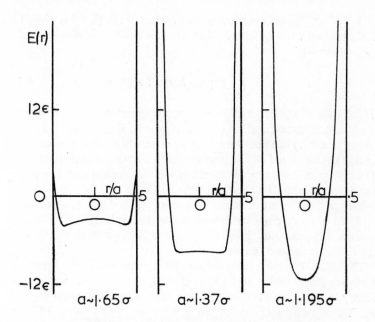

Fig. 6.2   The L.J.D. cell theory. The variation of $E(r)$ with r for three fluid densities. a is the nearest-neighbour distance

If only the 12 nearest neighbours are used to estimate Φ_L and $E(r)$ these have the values, for a nearest neighbour distance $a = \{\sqrt{2}\,V/N\}^{1/3}$ and a cell radius a_1,

$$\Phi_L = 6N\epsilon\left\{\left(\frac{N\sigma^3}{V}\right)^4 - 2\left(\frac{N\sigma^3}{V}\right)^2\right\} \quad \text{(c.f. eq. 4.26)} \qquad 6.37$$

and

$$E(r) = 12\epsilon\left\{\left(\frac{N\sigma^3}{V}\right)^4 \cdot l\left(\frac{r}{a_1}\right) - 2\left(\frac{N\sigma^3}{V}\right)^2 \cdot m\left(\frac{r}{a_1}\right)\right\} \qquad 6.38$$

where the functions $l(r/a_1)$ and $m(r/a_1)$ arise from integrating over all angular directions the potential of the 'smeared' molecules (assumption 3). They are given by

$$l(x) = (1 + 12x^2 + 25 \cdot 2x^4 + 12x^6 + x^8)(1 - x^2)^{-10} - 1 \qquad 6.39$$

$$m(x) = (1 + x^2)(1 - x^2)^{-4} - 1 \qquad 6.40$$

As before, the configurational free energy of the liquid is given by 6.32, but with the difference that the free volume is now (putting $dV_1 = 4\pi r^2 \, dr$)

$$V_f = \int_0^{a_1} \exp\left(-E(r)/kT\right)4\pi r^2 \, dr \qquad 6.41$$

The choice of the cell radius a_1 depends on what assumptions are made in the 'smearing' procedure. However, inspection of fig. 6.2 shows that $E(r)$ becomes large and positive when r approaches $0 \cdot 5a$, so that the integrand of 6.41 goes rapidly to zero beyond this distance. The choice of cell radius is therefore not too critical and Lennard–Jones and Devonshire took $a_1 = 0 \cdot 5a$.

We see that the introduction of a more realistic potential function leads to a more complex equation for the evaluation of the free energy. The necessary integrations are performed numerically and the results expressed in tabular form.

The most extensive calculations have been made by Wentorf, Buehler, Hirschfelder and Curtiss,[5] who have further refined the theory to allow for the effects of non-nearest neighbours on Φ_L and V_f. These authors chose for the cell radius a_1 the value $0 \cdot 5527a$, which makes the volume of the cell equal to the volume per molecule, i.e. they chose a_1 so that $\frac{4}{3}\pi a_1^3 = a^3/\sqrt{2}$.

The calculated equation of state proves to yield sinuous isothermals below a certain temperature and monotonic ones above. As a first, and severe, test of the extended L.J.D. theory we may see what predictions it makes about the critical constants. Identifying the critical point in the usual way, the following values are obtained:

$$p_c = 0 \cdot 434 \, \epsilon/\sigma^3; \qquad V_c = 1 \cdot 77 \, N\sigma^3; \qquad T_c = 1 \cdot 30 \, \epsilon/k \qquad 6.42$$

A comparison with the values from experiment, eq. 6.22, shows that T_c is about right, V_c is too small by a factor of almost two and p_c too large by a factor of almost four.

At the critical point the model of a molecule permanently confined in a cell is clearly rather implausible. We would expect the agreement with experiment to be better at the lower range of existence of the liquid range, the triple point. The triple point temperature is $0.70\ \epsilon/k$ for the heavier inert gases. Some configurational properties, i.e. those derived from $F_Q(N)$, for both liquid and solid argon, in reduced units, taken from the book by Barker,[6] are given below. The triple point pressure is so low that the molar volume may be obtained by setting $p = 0$ in the calculated equation of state.

TABLE 6.1

Configurational properties of argon at triple point, $T_r = 0.70\ \epsilon/k$

	$\left(\dfrac{\text{Volume}}{N\sigma^3}\right)$	$\left(\dfrac{\text{Internal}}{\substack{\text{energy}\\N\epsilon}}\right)$	$\left(\dfrac{\text{Entropy}}{Nk}\right)$	$\left(\dfrac{\substack{\text{Specific heat at}\\\text{const. volume}}}{Nk}\right)$
L.J.D. Theory	1·037	-7.32	-5.51	1·11
Exp. solid argon	1·035	-7.14	-5.33	1·41
Exp. liquid argon	1·186	-5.96	-3.64	0·85

On the whole, we see that the L.J.D. theory gives thermodynamic properties whose values are much closer to the experimental values for the *solid* than for the *liquid*. We shall discuss this more fully later. Meanwhile we must explain a serious difficulty which arises in all cell theories.

The problem of the communal free energy and entropy

Cell theories of liquids in which each cell is regarded as forming a separate thermodynamic system do not give the correct expression for the free energy or entropy. How this comes about may be made clear by treating the simple case of the ideal gas by the cell method.

For an ideal monatomic gas the complete and correct partition function and free energy are given by

$$Z = Z(N) = \left\{\frac{2\pi mkT}{h^2}\right\}^{3N/2} \frac{V^N}{N!}; \qquad F(N)\ \text{(correct)} = -kT \ln Z(N)$$
$$6.43$$

In the simple cell methods we regard the volume as divided into N cells by impenetrable walls, each cell being of volume V/N and containing just one molecule. The partition function for one cell is therefore obtained from 6.43 by replacing N by 1, and V by V/N giving

$$Z(1) = \left\{ \frac{2\pi mkT}{h^2} \right\}^{3/2} \cdot \left(\frac{V}{N} \right); \qquad F(1) \text{ (cell)} = -kT \ln Z(1) \quad 6.44$$

and the free energy of the N cells, regarded as N separate thermo-dynamic systems, is just $NF(1)$ (cell) or

$$F(N) \text{ (cell theory)} = -NkT \ln Z(1) = -kT \ln (Z(1))^N \qquad 6.45$$

If the cell model is correct this should give the same free energy as before, so the difference should vanish. On calculating the difference, denoted by ΔF, we find

$$\Delta F = F(N) \text{ (correct)} - F(N) \text{ (cell theory)} = -kT \ln \frac{Z(N)}{(Z(1))^N}$$
$$6.46$$

which, on putting in the values of $Z(1)$ and $Z(N)$, simplifies to

$$\Delta F = -kT \ln \left(\frac{N^N}{N!} \right) = -kT[N \ln N - \ln N!] \qquad 6.47$$

which is not zero. To estimate its value we may use Stirling's Theorem which states that when N is a large number the logarithm of its factorial approaches a value given by

$$\ln N! = N \ln N - N \qquad 6.48$$

And so

$$\Delta F = -NkT = -RT \quad \text{(for one mole)} \qquad 6.49$$

Thus the cell method gives a value for the free energy which, for an ideal gas, is RT units too high. Similarly the entropy $\Delta S = -(\partial \Delta F / \partial T)_V$ is R units too low. These errors are called the communal free energy and communal entropy, since they disappear when the walls of the cells are imagined removed so that all molecules have access to the common volume V.

This problem has given rise to much discussion. A crystal at low temperatures can be treated by what is essentially the cell method, in which each molecule is regarded as permanently confined to the neighbourhood of its lattice point (in the quantum-mechanical treatment this leads to Einstein's theory of solids). A gas at low densities certainly cannot be so treated. If a solid is first melted and then vaporised the communal free energy and entropy must appear at some stage. Lennard–Jones and Devonshire assumed that they appeared suddenly at the melting point, where, one may suppose, the molecules become free to move throughout the entire volume, and had the values appropriate to the ideal gas. They therefore added these values to their calculated results. Later investigations have shown this to be an oversimplification. In view of this uncertainty the comparisons with experimental data given above have been made with these corrections omitted.

In the simple cell theories given above we have supposed the volume to be divided into N cells, each containing one molecule. This procedure is by no means essential. One may divide up the volume in any arbitrary manner and this will affect the communal free energy and entropy. For example, we may divide it into a larger number of cells, some of which will be empty and some of which will contain one molecule. The empty cells may be called holes, and hole theories of liquids are based on the idea that a fluid can be regarded as a mixture of molecules and holes to which statistical methods can be applied.[7] Thus a molecule in an occupied cell may be regarded as surrounded not by twelve nearest-neighbours but by a lesser number. For liquid argon near the triple point the X-ray and neutron diffraction data suggest that this number may be eight to ten, depending on how one determines the limits of area to be associated with the first peak in fig. 3.2. We may then put the number of nearest-neighbours equal to $12(1-\omega)$ where 12ω is the number of holes, or adjacent unoccupied cells, and ω is a new parameter to be evaluated. The potential energy of a wanderer in an occupied cell may then be approximated to $(1-\omega)$ times the L.J.D. nearest-neighbour value. The free volume is more difficult to evaluate since it clearly depends on the number and arrangement of the holes. At this point in hole theories one must choose some reasonably simple equation to relate ω and V_f.

The advantage of hole theories is that, as the parameter ω varies from zero to unity, the configurational integral varies continuously also, from the correct form for the solid to the correct form for a gas, so that the communal problems do not arise. The disadvantage of hole theories is that the relation between V_f and ω is often frankly empirical, or justified by physical arguments of varying degrees of plausibility. Hole theories may be regarded as extensions of the L.J.D. theory but the practical improvements they make to that theory are not sufficiently striking to warrant further discussion here.

An alternative choice is to modify our cell model to allow for multiple occupation of the cells. This also reduces the communal errors, as again may be seen most clearly for the ideal gas. Suppose, for example, we divide the volume into a number, K, of larger cells of equal volume, and suppose further that these cells contain the same number, r, of molecules, where $Kr = N$. The volume of each cell is then V/K or rV/N. If we regard each cell as a separate thermodynamic system our partition function for one cell is obtained from the general expression 6.43, by replacing $3N/2$ by $3r/2$, V^N by $(rV/N)^r$, and $N!$ by $r!$. The free energy of the whole liquid is then K, or N/r, times the free energy of one cell. If we follow through an easy calculation similar to the preceding one we find for the communal free energy of one mole

$$\Delta F = -RT\left\{1+\frac{(\ln r!)}{r}-\ln r\right\} \qquad 6.50$$

For $r = 1$ this gives $\Delta F = -RT$, as before. For $r = 2$, $\Delta F = -0.653RT$, so the error is reduced. For $r = 10$ we get $\Delta F = -0.21RT$ and when r is large enough to permit the use of Stirling's theorem, $\ln r! = r \ln r - r$, we find $\Delta F = 0$. Unfortunately, for real fluids, when r is greater than unity, the evaluation of the cell free energy becomes exceedingly difficult or impossible.

The errors which arise in the cell method may be summarised as follows. To evaluate the thermodynamic properties correctly the configuration integral must be evaluated for every possible spatial arrangement of the molecules, each weighted with the Boltzmann factor $\exp(-\Phi/kT)$. In attempting this task we are quite free, if we wish, to divide the volume into smaller units in *imagination* by the *concept* of cell walls. Provided these walls are only mental concepts, the molecules can, as it were, move freely in and out of the cells so that a cell may contain any number of molecules. The correct configurational partition function for the fluid will then be obtained if we sum over all possible probability distributions of the N molecules among, and in, the cells. If, however, we suppose the walls to have a physical reality, we necessarily prevent the exchange of molecules between the cells and thus exclude all configurations except those which can be realised with the postulated original distribution of the molecules among the cells. Furthermore, if we regard each cell as an independent thermodynamic system, we are really implying that the molecules in a cell do not exert forces on molecules in neighbouring cells or, in technical language, we are neglecting *correlation* effects between the molecules in different cells. These two assumptions give rise to the communal free energy and entropy errors. For an ideal gas only the first effect exists. The communal free energy then depends only on the temperature and not on the volume, so that neither the ordinary or caloric equation of state is affected. For a real fluid strong correlation effects are also present, and we must expect that the communal free energy will depend on both volume and temperature and hence will affect all the thermodynamic properties.

From a geometrical point of view the lattice-like cell model brings back into our picture of a fluid just that feature of long-range order whose absence in real fluids constitutes the essential difference between a solid and a fluid. A well-known rule in thermodynamics is that the greater the degree of order in a system the less the entropy, so it is not surprising that the cell model gives values for the entropy which are too low. As cell theories have become increasingly refined, and as more experimental data of higher accuracy have accumulated, it is becoming clear that cell theories are, in their simple forms at least, excellent classical descriptions of the solid state, that is, of expanded lattice structures at high temperatures, rather than descriptions of the liquid state. Ways in which these limitations of cell theories can be removed have been proposed by de Boer, Pople and Barker,[7] but so far numerical results from these new approaches are meagre.

From the point of view of the experimental physicist the communal problem may be interpreted as follows. To determine the free energy, or any extensive thermodynamic property for one mole, it is not necessary to make measurements on exactly one mole. We may make our measurements on, say, one-tenth of a mole and multiply the result by ten, or on one-hundredth of a mole and multiply by one hundred. That is, we may legitimately divide our original mole into a relatively small number of equal parts, constituting separate thermodynamic systems, make measurements on one of these systems, and scale up the results. If this process of subdivision is carried too far, however, an error will begin to appear. In small samples the number of molecules near the surface of the fluid, or near the walls of the container, becomes a larger proportion of the total number in the sample. These surface molecules lack fluid molecules on one side, and hence are in a different local environment with a different potential energy, compared with interior molecules. In very small samples (presuming we could make accurate measurements on them) these errors become large. In our simple cell theories we have carried the process to its limit, of just one molecule per cell. Such allowances as we have made for interactions between the systems, or cells, are not adequate to correct for errors which appear in the subdivision process. We may expect that the communal errors will begin to become significant for a sample whose linear dimensions become comparable with the extent of the short-range order in liquids, say two or three times σ. It is readily calculated that such a sample would contain some dozens of molecules.

If we could apply statistical methods to such a sample we might expect to get a much more accurate estimate for the thermodynamic properties than our simple cell model can give. In the next chapter we shall see how the development of fast electronic computers has opened up an approach along these lines.

7

MONTE CARLO AND MOLECULAR DYNAMICS

METHODS

The molecules in fluids are in ceaseless random motion, constantly changing their positions and velocities. With the aid of fast electronic computers it is possible to set up a mathematical model which imitates this motion for systems containing a limited number of molecules, some tens or hundreds. The kinetic and thermodynamic properties of this model can be calculated by the computer and the results compared with experiment. The calculations are, in effect, experiments performed on the model rather than on a real physical system.

The Monte Carlo method[1, 5]
In this method the configurational thermodynamic properties of the model are calculated by the methods of statistical mechanics.

The centre square of fig. 7.1 represents, in two dimensions, a random configuration of molecules. For the moment we ignore the molecules in surrounding squares. With the aid of a Cartesian coordinate system we may specify the positions of the molecules in the centre square by coordinates (x_1, y_1), (x_2, y_2), etc. To imitate the motion of the molecules the computer is programmed so as to 'move' one molecule at a time in accordance with certain rules, thereby generating new configurations. When a large number of configurations have been generated, the configurational properties can be averaged over them.

To generate a new configuration the computer selects one molecule, say that labelled i with coordinates x_i, y_i and 'moves' it to a new position x_i', y_i' where

$$x_i' = x_i + \alpha\,\Delta \qquad y_i' = y_i + \beta\,\Delta \qquad\qquad 7.1$$

Here α and β are two random decimal numbers, generated by the machine, which lie in the range -1 to $+1$, and Δ is the maximum

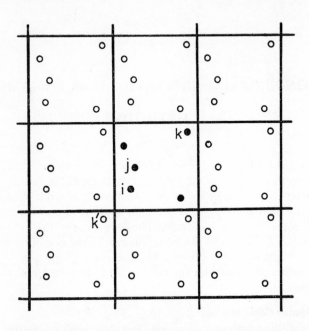

Fig. 7.1 The Monte Carlo method in two dimensions. A random configuration of molecules in the central square is surrounded by identical 'ghost' systems. For clarity, only five molecules are shown in each square

allowed displacement per move which, for the moment, we may regard as arbitrary.

For any configuration, the computer can calculate the distance, r_{ij}, between the pair i, j, knowing their coordinates. With a known intermolecular potential function $\phi(r_{ij})$ it can then find the potential energy of the configuration $\Phi = \sum_{\text{pairs}} \phi(r_{ij})$ and then the Boltzmann factor $\exp(-\Phi/kT)$, for any chosen temperature T.

From this point on an obvious procedure would be to calculate the thermodynamic properties by the Method of Averages. If the average of the configurational potential energy itself is required, for example, use would be made of the formula (for the three-dimensional case)

$$U_{pot} = \bar{\Phi} = \frac{\int \Phi \exp(-\Phi/kT)\, dV_1 \ldots dV_N}{\int \exp(-\Phi/kT)\, dV_1 \ldots dV_N} \qquad 7.2$$

which can readily be derived from 5.43 by factoring out the momentum part. If we remember that an integral represents the limit of a summation process we see that this can be written

$$U_{pot} = \bar{\Phi} = \frac{\sum \Phi \exp(-\Phi/kT)}{\sum \exp(-\Phi/kT)} \qquad 7.3$$

where the summations are taken over a large number of configurations, great enough to effectively exhaust all possible spatial configurations of the molecules.

However, there is a difficulty in this procedure. Because of the close packing of molecules an arbitrary displacement of a molecule according to the rule of eq. 7.1 will very often bring it so close to one or more of its neighbours that the repulsive forces cause the potential energy to become very large and positive—the molecules 'overlap'. The Boltzmann factor then becomes effectively zero for a very high proportion of all the configurations generated, and the method becomes impracticable. A modification of the method of averages is therefore made, using a procedure developed by Metropolis[1] and his collaborators. Starting with the molecules in a configuration numbered, say, m in the series, the computer calculates the *change* in Φ, say $\Delta\Phi$, produced by the next move. If $\Delta\Phi$ is negative the next configuration is a new one. If $\Delta\Phi$ is positive the computer evaluates $\exp(-\Delta\Phi/kT)$, which will lie between 0 and 1. The machine then selects a random decimal number in the range 0 to 1, and compares the exponential with it. If the exponential is the greater the move is allowed and the next configuration is a different one, say n. If the exponential is the lesser the move is disallowed, the molecule returned to its old position, and the next configuration is again m. This procedure prevents excessive overlapping. One might say that the computer requires the molecule to bounce back to its original position if it comes too close to its neighbours. Whatever happens, the value of the potential energy, or any other function of the coordinates of interest, is calculated for the resulting configuration. The next molecule is then moved and the process repeated. In the early work the molecules were moved in turn, in later work the next molecule to be moved was selected at random.

It can be shown from the mathematical theory of random processes that, with this modification, the frequency of occurrences of a configuration of energy Φ will become proportional to $\exp(-\Phi/kT)$ when the number of configurations in the series becomes very large. Thus, instead of selecting configurations at random and weighting them with a factor $\exp(-\Phi/kT)$, the procedure is to select configurations with a frequency proportional to $\exp(-\Phi/kT)$ and weight them equally. It is this modification which prevents, incidentally, a direct calculation of the partition function.

With the new procedure the mean value of any function of coordinates, say $G(x_i, y_i, x_j, y_j, \ldots)$, is given by

$$\bar{G} = \frac{1}{L} \sum_{n=1}^{n=L} G_n \qquad\qquad 7.4$$

where G_n is the value of G for the nth configuration in a long series of L. The most important averages are those of Φ itself, which gives the potential part of the internal energy and so the caloric equation of state, and that of the virial of the intermolecular forces, $\frac{1}{3}\sum_{\text{pairs}} r_{ij} \cdot F(r_{ij})$, which (eq. 5.22) gives the ordinary equation of state.

The magnitude of Δ, the maximum allowed displacement, must be chosen as a compromise between two extremes. If Δ is too large most moves will be forbidden, if too small the configuration does not change much between moves. In either case too long a time is required for proper averaging.

For molecules interacting with the L.J. 6–12 potential an I.B.M. computer generates about 19,000 configurations per hour for a system of 32 molecules, and about 6500 configurations per hour for a system of 108 molecules. For proper averaging about 50,000 configurations are needed. The length of the side of the square (cube) and the number of molecules it contains determines the number–density of the system, and the temperature appears in the Boltzmann factor so that comparisons can be made between a real fluid and the model.

Two further difficulties arise. With such a relatively small number of molecules the surface effects, discussed at the end of the last chapter, are important. To partially correct for these it is supposed, in programming the computer, that the central square of fig. 7.1 is surrounded on all sides by many copies of itself containing exactly the same configuration of molecules, which move in unison with the central set. These molecules are sometimes called 'ghosts' of the central set. Errors due to surface effects are then minimised by employing the following rule. To calculate any property of pairs formed by molecule i and the others j, k ... etc., the distance between i and either j, k, ... or one of j, k ... s 'ghosts' is used, whichever is the shorter. Thus in fig. 7.1 the computer would calculate for the pair i and j in the same cell, but would calculate for i and k' since the 'ghost' k' is nearer i than k itself. This artifice also solves the second difficulty, which arises whenever a molecule suffers a displacement which takes it out of the central square, for then its 'ghost' automatically enters the square through the opposite side. It will be seen that this correction for surface effects is equivalent to an attempt to allow for correlation effects in the cell theories.

The radial distribution function can be obtained from the molecular coordinates in any configuration by calculating the numbers of pairs of molecules whose centres lie within a specified range of separations and averaging the results over all configurations.

The method of molecular dynamics[2]

A way of following in detail the motion of a limited number of molecules would be to solve their equations of motion, that is, to equate the instantaneous force on a molecule, due to all the others located at known positions, to its mass times its acceleration and then solve all the simultaneous equations so obtained to give the trajectories of the particles. This is the so-called many-body problem and cannot be solved analytically, indeed it is impossible to obtain a solution for only three bodies in the general case. If, however, we restrict ourselves to very simple laws of intermolecular force it is possible, with the aid of a computer, to trace out the molecular trajectories for a limited number (some hundreds) of molecules. This is the method of molecular dynamics.

The simplest model of a molecule is the perfectly elastic hard sphere, for which most computations have been made. Suppose we start a number, N, of such spheres from known positions in a box specified by Cartesian coordinates, with initial velocities which are, say, all equal in magnitude but which are distributed in direction in a specified manner. Velocities are then changed only when one sphere collides with another; in between collisions the molecules travel in straight lines with constant speed. By a sufficiently fine division of our time scale it is therefore possible to represent the molecular interactions as a rapid succession of two-body collisions. For a two-body collision the new velocities after impact can be calculated, in magnitude and direction, from simple equations obtained by applying the laws of conservation of momentum and energy to the collision process.

In programming the computer the first object is to decide in what order collisions will occur. The first collision may take place between any one of the N spheres and one of the $(N-1)$ others, giving $N(N-1)/2$ possibilities. To reduce the labour of examining all these it is possible to apply simple tests which show, for example, that the centres of a particular pair of molecules are receding or, if they are approaching, will never come as close as a molecular diameter, or that they are so far apart that the time which will elapse before the collision is long compared with the times for many other collisions. In this way a number of collisions can be put in a sequence in the order of their expected collision times. The computer then calculates the new velocities and directions for each collision and applies tests to see whether these new velocities will upset the expected sequence. If so, the original sequence is suitably re-ordered. When a complete sequence has been worked out, a new sequence is set up and a further cycle of collisions calculated. To minimise surface effects the same device of 'ghost' systems is employed as in the Monte Carlo method.

An I.B.M. 704 computer can calculate about 2000 collisions per hour for a system of 100 hard spheres. As each collision involves two spheres this corresponds to an average of 40 collisions per sphere per hour. As the calculation proceeds the dynamical history of each sphere is recorded on magnetic tape and it is also possible to display the 'molecular' motion on a cathode-ray oscillograph. Thus, as well as being able to evaluate statistical averages for the system the individual motion of every sphere can be studied in detail, if desired.

Systems of hard spheres when not in contact do not, of course, possess any mutual potential energy so that those thermodynamic properties of real fluids which depend on the potential energy are not obtainable. The equation of state, however, can be obtained by slightly modifying the virial of 5.22 to a form suitable for elastic collisions. One replaces the force $F(r_{ij})$ on a colliding sphere by the impulsive change in momentum and then averages the time rate of change over the system. The temperature is determined by the mean kinetic energy of the spheres, which remains constant and equal to the known initial kinetic energy. The radial distribution function can also be obtained from averages of the molecular coordinates.

The method of molecular dynamics is complementary to the Monte Carlo method, which has also been applied to hard spheres. Molecular dynamics can, however, also be used to study non-equilibrium behaviour by choosing appropriate initial conditions.[3] For example, the molecules may be started off bunched together in a small region and the subsequent 'explosion' followed as they expand to fill the box. Or a number of neighbouring molecules may be started with initial velocities higher than the remainder, and the decay of this 'hot spot' followed as its energy is dissipated throughout the system. It is found that thermodynamic equilibrium is generally attained after a relatively small number of collisions, on average about four for each molecule. Although the hard-sphere model of a molecule is not a very realistic one, many theoretical investigations in mathematical physics, particularly in the kinetic theory of gases, employ the model, so that molecular dynamics permits illuminating comparisons with these theories. Molecular dynamics calculations have also been made for the 'square well' intermolecular potential function in which the effect of attractive forces is allowed for to some extent.

Results

The equation of state of a system of hard spheres calculated in different ways is shown in fig. 7.2. The molecular dynamics results are due to Wainwright and Alder and are shown as a solid curve. Results from the simple cell theory (eq. 6.29) are shown, together with those obtained from Mayer's cluster expansion method, that is, the virial equation of state with the five known virial coefficients. The volume V_0 is the volume of the close-packed lattice structure when the spheres are in contact, the highest possible density of packing.

As this limiting density is approached, the simple cell theory gives results which agree with the molecular dynamics method. At these densities the cluster expansion method cannot be expected to be convergent, the fact that the dotted curve lies near the others is accidental. At larger volumes it will be seen that the molecular dynamics method gives two curves. The explanation for this is obtained from an examination of the 'molecular' motion. If the 'molecules' are started from a regular lattice arrangement and the density is high the lattice structure persists, each 'molecule' making small random movements near its lattice point. At lower densities the system may remain in the ordered state for some time, but then makes an abrupt

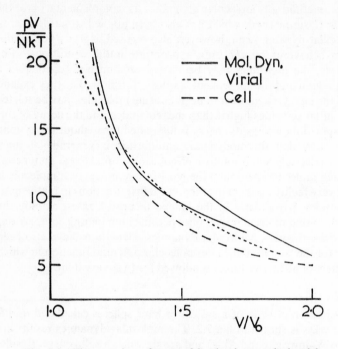

Fig. 7.2   The equation of state of hard spheres calculated by three different methods. V_0 is the volume of the close-packed solid

transition, revealed by a sudden increase in the pressure. At a transition the 'molecules' are seen to leave their lattice point and diffuse irregularly throughout the box, and the system remains in the disordered state. By starting the molecules from lattice or disordered states two separate curves can be obtained over a limited range of densities. At a rather sharply-defined density region, near $V/V_0 =$ 1·525, occasional transitions in both directions between ordered and disordered states can be obtained, but these are rare, perhaps only 0 to 3 in 30 hours of calculating time.

It must, therefore, be concluded that the upper solid curve obtained at large volumes refers to the fluid and the lower, extending to small volumes, to the solid. In the fluid region the simple cell theory and the virial equation give results which lie below the molecular dynamics data. The Monte Carlo results for rigid spheres are in agreement with the molecular dynamics, though in some of the early work

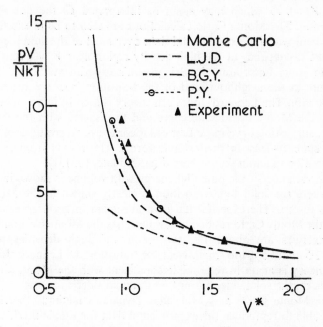

Fig. 7.3 pV/NkT as a function of V^* at $T^* = 2.74$ for an L.J. 6–12 fluid, according to four theories

there was a puzzling discrepancy as the runs were not long enough to reveal the solid–fluid transition.

For molecules interacting with the more realistic L.J. 6–12 potential, Wood and Parker[5] have made Monte Carlo calculations for a reduced temperature of $T^* = 2.74$ ($=kT/\epsilon$) and over a range of reduced volumes V^* from 0.75 to 7.5 ($V^* = V/N\sigma^3$). This temperature is about twice the critical temperature and the range of reduced volumes corresponds to a range of density from about two-fifths to four times the critical density. The calculations therefore refer to the highly compressed gas (and solid, see below) and not to the liquid, though the range of density extends above the normal liquid density.

The equation of state for this temperature is shown in fig. 7.3 together with the predictions of three other theories. For comparison with experiment there are compressibility data on argon (for which $T^* = 2.74$ corresponds to 55°C) due to Michels and to Bridgmann. The Monte Carlo results lie on two distinct curves with a break near $V^* = 0.95$ which may again be interpreted as the gas–solid transition. The Monte Carlo calculations are seen to be in excellent agreement with the experimental data over most of the fluid region, and the discrepancy at the high density region near $V^* = 1$ may be due to some uncertainty in Bridgmann's experimental data. The pressure in the neighbourhood of the transition is of the order of 10,000 atm. The Lennard–Jones cell theory is seen to join smoothly on to the Monte Carlo *solid* curve and to disagree with the *liquid* curve, suggesting once more that cell theories are descriptions of the solid state, at least in their simple forms. The results from radial distribution function theories are discussed later (p. 131).

The variation of the potential energy with volume is shown in fig. 7.4 where the solid–fluid transition is clearly shown in the Monte Carlo results. The experimental data are again in good agreement with the Monte Carlo results; at low densities the Monte Carlo internal energies are about 1% too small and high densities near $V^* = 1.5$ about 5% too small. Near the transition the Lennard–Jones cell theory is again in reasonable agreement with the Monte Carlo results on the solid side, but not on the fluid side.

The Monte Carlo and Molecular Dynamics methods therefore seem able to reproduce the experimental data for simple fluids with remarkable accuracy. The Monte Carlo method is probably the best means at our disposal at present for studying the properties of fluids at high densities and pressures. Calculations for the true liquid region have not been made so far. The equilibrium vapour pressure for liquids at temperatures well below the critical is much smaller than the range of pressures covered in the above calculations. These low pressures are, as we shall see, extremely sensitive to any uncertainty in the calculations. The chief approximation in the Monte Carlo method is probably the use of the minimum distance rule for correcting for surface effects. Changing the size of the cell and the number of molecules it contains in such a way as to keep the density constant enables this effect to be studied. It appears that little error arises in the calculated thermodynamic properties except possibly near a phase transition. The relatively small numbers of molecules that can be handled and the periodic nature of the boundary conditions (neighbouring cells reproduce the configuration in the central cell)

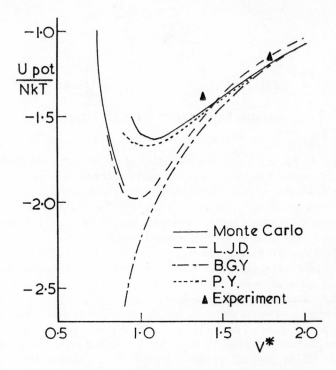

Fig. 7.4 The potential energy, in molecular reduced units, of a L.J. 6–12 fluid at $T^*=2.74$ as a function of V^*, according to four theories

may tend to produce a phase transition at a volume different from that in a real fluid. The only other disadvantage is a more prosaic one; Monte Carlo calculations and the like involve long and costly use of expensive computers and a great deal of calculation is necessary to produce an extensive range of numerical data.

5

8

THE METHOD OF THE RADIAL

DISTRIBUTION FUNCTION

A third approach to an understanding of the properties of fluids is based on attempts to calculate the radial distribution function, $\rho(r)$. For fluids whose molecules interact with central additive forces an accurate knowledge of $\rho(r)$ for all temperatures and densities would give us the thermodynamic properties, via the ordinary and caloric equations of state, as we now proceed to show.

To find the caloric equation of state we need to calculate the molecular potential energy. This may be found by simple reasoning based on an integration process, analogous to the lattice summation procedure used for crystals, as follows.

Suppose we select one molecule as our origin of coordinates and calculate the mutual potential energy between this molecule and those in a spherical shell lying between r and $r + \delta r$. The average number of molecules in this shell is $\rho(r)4\pi r^2 \, \delta r$. For an intermolecular potential function $\phi(r)$ the mutual potential energy is then $\phi(r) . \rho(r) . 4\pi r^2 \delta r$. To find the total potential energy of the fluid we then (a) integrate this expression over all values of r, (b) imagine the calculation repeated for each of the N molecules chosen as the centre molecule, giving just N times the result and (c) divide the answer by two to correct for the counting of each pair of molecules twice. We thus obtain

$$U_{\text{pot}} = \overline{\Phi} = \frac{N}{2} \int_0^\infty \phi(r) . \rho(r) . 4\pi r^2 \, \mathrm{d}r \qquad 8.1$$

where, because of the rapid approach to zero of $\phi(r)$ with distance, we may take the upper limit of the integral as infinity. In the calculation we have supposed that all molecules have the same local environment so that $\rho(r)$ is independent of the origin. For molecules near the surface of the fluid this will not be true,† but in a macroscopic quantity of fluid the proportion of these surface molecules is negligible.

To get the total internal energy we add the kinetic energy to the above expression. For a monatomic fluid this is $\frac{3}{2}NkT$, giving the caloric equation of state,

$$U = \frac{3}{2}NkT + \frac{N}{2}\int_0^\infty \phi(r).\rho(r).4\pi r^2\, dr \qquad 8.2$$

To find the ordinary equation of state we make use of Clausius' virial theorem

$$pV = NkT + \frac{1}{3}\overline{\sum_{\text{pairs}} F(r_{ij})r_{ij}} \qquad 5.22$$

where i and j are two molecules. Choose i as the central molecule and j as one of the molecules in the spherical shell. Then $r_{ij}=r$ and $F(r_{ij})=F(r)=-d\phi(r)/dr$. The contribution to the summation in the virial of the molecules in the shell is then $-\frac{1}{3}r(d\phi(r)/dr)4\pi r^2 \rho(r)\, dr$ and by similar reasoning to that used before in (a), (b) and (c) we get

$$p = \frac{NkT}{V} - \frac{N}{6V}\int_0^\infty \frac{d\phi(r)}{dr}\rho(r).4\pi r^3\, dr \qquad 8.3$$

Equations 8.2 and 8.3 can also be derived by more formal methods.[1]

In the partition function method we obtained the equations of state by appropriate differentiations of the free energy. In the present method we can obtain the free energy by reversing these calculations and deriving the free energy from appropriate integrations. Thus the only unknown quantity of importance in this approach is $\rho(r)$.

As $\rho(r)$ can be obtained from diffraction experiments it might be thought that immediate calculations of U and p are possible. Unfortunately the accuracy with which $\rho(r)$ is at present known is quite inadequate for this purpose. The great sensitivity of the pressure, for example, to $\rho(r)$ when calculated from 8.3 may be seen by taking a

† The study of these surface effects leads to a molecular theory of surface tension.

typical case. For one mole of liquid argon at its triple point, $T = 83 \cdot 8°K$, $V = 0 \cdot 0281$ litre mole^{-1}, whence NkT/V is some 245 atm. The experimental triple point pressure is only 0·6 atm. Therefore the integral term in 8.3 must be about $-244 \cdot 4$ atm. Pressures calculated theoretically from 8.3 will therefore depend on the difference of two large and nearly equal quantities, so that even a slight uncertainty in $\rho(r)$ will lead to severe errors. At the critical point the situation is not so bad, here NkT/V is 166 atm while the experimental critical pressure is 48 atm, so the integral term must be -118 atm.

We must therefore attempt to calculate $\rho(r)$ from first principles. This is equivalent to determining the configurational pair distribution function n_2 since this is directly related to $\rho(r)$ by 5.51. We consider first, however, the general configurational distribution, n_h, for a small number, h, of molecules.

The expression for n_h is obtained from 5.47 and 5.45. We may write it a little more economically by noting that the integral in the denominator of 5.45 is the same as the one which occurs in the definition of $Q(N)$, eq. 6.5. Combining these equations we obtain

$$n_h = \frac{1}{(N-h)! Q(N)} \int \exp(-\beta\Phi) \, dV_{h+1} \ldots dV_N \qquad 8.4$$

Let us try to give a physical meaning to this equation. We first imagine a static configuration of all the N molecules in which each volume element $dV_1, dV_2, \ldots, dV_N$ contains a molecule. The quantity Φ is the total potential energy of this configuration. We now imagine that the positions of volume elements numbered 1 to h (and the molecules they contain) are kept fixed, while the remaining molecules are allowed to move and to take up every possible spatial configuration, so that all the volume elements dV_{h+1} to dV_N range over the entire volume of the container. The integral then represents a summation and averaging process which exhausts all possible probability distributions. To indicate which volume elements are supposed to be held fixed we extend our notation slightly and write $n_h = n_h (1, 2, \ldots, h)$.

In particular, the pair distribution function for fixed volume elements dV_1 and dV_2 is

$$n_2 (1, 2) = \frac{1}{(N-2)! Q(N)} \int \exp(-\beta\Phi) \, dV_3 \ldots dV_N \qquad 8.5$$

The (multiple) integrals in the above expression are just as intractable as the integrals in the configurational partition function. Let us see if we can side-step the need to evaluate them by following a procedure due in its essentials to Yvon, Born and Green.[2] This is to investigate what change occurs in $n_2 (1, 2)$ when we vary the position of the volume element dV_1 (and the molecule it contains) by a small displacement, say in the x-direction, so that the x-coordinate of the molecule in δV_1 becomes $x_1 + dx_1$. During this displacement the molecule in dV_2 is to be kept fixed. The effect of this change on $n_2(1, 2)$ is then, from 8.5,

$$\frac{\partial n_2(1, 2)}{\partial x_1} = \frac{1}{(N-2)! Q(N)} \frac{\partial}{\partial x_1} \int \exp(-\beta\Phi) \, dV_3 \ldots dV_N \qquad 8.6$$

Now Φ depends on x_1 (and all other coordinates) but the variables of integration do not. We may therefore differentiate under the integral sign to give

$$\frac{\partial n_2(1, 2)}{\partial x_1} = \frac{1}{(N-2)! Q(N)} \int \exp(-\beta\Phi) \left(-\beta \frac{\partial\Phi}{\partial x_1}\right) dV_3 \ldots dV_N \qquad 8.7$$

To calculate $\partial\Phi/\partial x_1$ let us write out some of the terms on which it depends:

$$\Phi = \phi_{12} + \phi_{13} + \cdots \phi_{1N} + \phi_{23} + \phi_{24} + \cdots + \cdots \qquad 8.8$$

where the pairs of suffixes label the corresponding volume elements. The first $N-1$ terms of this sum depend on the coordinates of molecule 1, but the remainder do not. These last will therefore disappear in the differentiation. Of those that remain we keep the first, $\partial\phi_{12}/\partial x_1$, separate and group the remainder together to give

$$\frac{\partial\Phi}{\partial x_1} = \frac{\partial\phi_{12}}{\partial x_1} + \sum_{k=3}^{N} \frac{\partial\phi_{1k}}{\partial x_1} \qquad 8.9$$

On putting this expression in 8.7 we obtain

$$\frac{\partial n_2(1, 2)}{\partial x_1} = \frac{-\beta}{(N-2)! Q(N)} \int \frac{\partial\phi_{12}}{\partial x_1} \exp(-\beta\Phi) \, dV_3 \ldots dV_N$$

$$- \frac{\beta}{(N-2)! Q(N)} \int \sum_{k=3}^{N} \frac{\partial\phi_{1k}}{\partial x_1} \exp(-\beta\Phi) \, dV_3 \ldots dV_N \qquad 8.10$$

In the first term on the right-hand side the quantity $\partial\phi_{12}/\partial x_1$ does not depend on the variables of integration and so can be treated as a constant and taken outside the integral. On comparing this term with 8.5 we see that it is then just $-\beta(\partial\phi_{12}/\partial x_1)n_2(1, 2)$. The second expression on the right of 8.10 is the sum of $(N-2)$ terms, one for each value of k from 3 to N. The first of these is

$$-\frac{\beta}{(N-2)!Q(N)} \int \frac{\partial\phi_{13}}{\partial x_1} \exp(-\beta\Phi) \, \mathrm{d}V_3 \ldots \mathrm{d}V_N \qquad 8.11$$

where we remind ourselves that the single integral sign represents repeated integrations over the variables V_3 to V_N. Suppose now we first integrate over the whole ranges of the variables V_4 to V_N, keeping V_3 fixed. During these integrations $\partial\phi_{13}/\partial x_1$ can therefore be treated as a constant. We may indicate this order of procedure by writing 8.11 as

$$-\frac{\beta}{(N-2)!Q(N)} \int_{V3} \frac{\partial\phi_{13}}{\partial x_1} \left[\int \exp(-\beta\Phi) \, \mathrm{d}V_4 \ldots \mathrm{d}V_N \right] \mathrm{d}V_3 \qquad 8.12$$

where the integrations in the square brackets are to be performed first. Now if we put $h=3$ in eq. 8.4 we see that the square bracket in 8.12 is closely related to the triplet distribution function. In fact, it is $n_3(1, 2, 3)(N-3)!Q(N)$. Thus, since $(N-2)!=(N-2)(N-3)!$, 8.12 simplifies to

$$-\frac{\beta}{(N-2)} \int \frac{\partial\phi_{13}}{\partial x_1} n_3(1, 2, 3) \, \mathrm{d}V_3 \qquad 8.13$$

In a similar way the term corresponding to $k=4$ of the summation in 8.10 is

$$-\frac{\beta}{(N-2)} \int \frac{\partial\phi_{14}}{\partial x_1} n_3(1, 2, 4) \, \mathrm{d}V_4 \qquad 8.14$$

This, however, must be just the same as 8.13, as may be seen as follows. The variables V_3 or V_4 are to range over the entire volume in each expression, and the molecule in $\mathrm{d}V_3$ is indistinguishable in its properties from that in $\mathrm{d}V_4$. If we could evaluate these integrals, the variables V_3 and V_4 would disappear, leaving, therefore, only the same function of the coordinates of $\mathrm{d}V_1$ and $\mathrm{d}V_2$. Alternatively, we may argue that the value of a definite integral cannot depend on the particular mathematical symbol we employ for the variable, so whether we choose to call the variable V_3 or V_4 is immaterial. By the same argument all the terms in the summation in 8.10 have the same value as 8.13. There are $(N-2)$ of these in all, which factor just cancels the $(N-2)$ in the denominator of 8.13. Our equation 8.10 finally becomes

$$\frac{\partial n_2(1, 2)}{\partial x_1} = -\beta n_2(1, 2) \frac{\partial \phi_{12}}{\partial x_1} - \beta \int \frac{\partial \phi_{13}}{\partial x_1} n_3(1, 2, 3) \, dV_3 \qquad 8.15$$

This equation states that the change in the pair distribution function $n_2(1, 2)$ due to a small displacement of molecule 1, keeping molecule 2 fixed, is the sum of two parts. The first of these arises from the direct force, $-\partial \phi_{12}/\partial x_1$, exerted by molecule 2 on molecule 1. The second arises from the forces exerted by all the other molecules averaged over all their possible configurations.

In this equation we know β $(=1/kT)$ and the pair potential ϕ_{12}. Moreover, the integral in 8.15 is not a complex multiple integral but a comparatively simple one, over V_3 only. Nevertheless it seems that our mathematical exertions have been largely wasted, for in trying to derive a reasonably simple equation for $n_2(1, 2)$ we have obtained an expression in which the unknown triplet function has made its appearance, and the expression for $n_3(1, 2, 3)$ brings us back to an intractable multiple integral. We may, by an analogous calculation, try to find an expression for $\partial n_3(1, 2, 3)/\partial x_1$ but this leads to an equation depending on the next higher function, $n_4(1, 2, 3, 4)$, and so on.

In order to make progress we must break this chain of linked equations by introducing a simplifying assumption, and at this point, therefore, we abandon a rigorous attempt to calculate the pair distribution. The assumption was put forward by Kirkwood in 1935 and is known as the Superposition Approximation. It is to approximate the triplet function by a product of pair functions

$$n_3(1, 2, 3) = [n_2(1, 2) \, n_2(2, 3) \, n_2(3, 1)]/\rho_0^3 \qquad 8.16$$

The physical nature of this assumption can be seen as follows. The probability of any configuration of potential energy Φ is proportional to the Boltzmann factor, $\exp(-\beta\Phi)$. If molecules 1 and 2 are very close together ϕ_{12} will be very large and the variation of $n_2(1, 2)$ with separation will be dominated by the variation of ϕ_{12}, the remaining, more distant, molecules exerting only a minor effect. Hence at close distances $n_2(1, 2) \propto \exp(-\beta\phi_{12})$. Similarly, if three molecules are very close to each other the probability of the configuration

$n_3(1, 2, 3)$ will be determined largely by the mutual potential energy of these three, which is $\phi_{12} + \phi_{23} + \phi_{31}$. Hence

$$n_3(1, 2, 3) \propto \exp -\beta(\phi_{12} + \phi_{23} + \phi_{31})$$
$$\text{or} \quad \propto \exp -\beta\phi_{12}.\exp -\beta\phi_{23}.\exp -\beta\phi_{31}$$

that is, $n_3(1, 2, 3) \propto n_2(1, 2).n_2(2, 3).n_2(3, 1)$. On the other hand, when all three molecules are widely separated each pair function becomes ρ_0^2, while the triplet function becomes $N(N-1)(N-2)/V^3$ or effectively ρ_0^3. The superposition approximation therefore correctly expresses the relation between the pair and triplet functions for these extreme cases.

When we use the superposition approximation for $n_3(1, 2, 3)$ in 8.15 we can remove $n_2(1, 2)$ outside the integral to give

$$\frac{\partial n_2(1, 2)}{\partial x_1} = -\beta n_2(1, 2) \frac{\partial \phi_{12}}{\partial x_1} - \frac{\beta n_2(1, 2)}{\rho_0^3} \int \frac{\partial \phi_{13}}{\partial x_1} n_2(2, 3)n_2(3, 1) \, \mathrm{d}V_3$$

$$8.17$$

This equation involves only pair distributions, so we have broken the chain of equations which leads to the higher order functions.

The further developments will be indicated only in outline, since the argument from now on is one of mathematics rather than physics. First, we write down equations for displacements of the molecule in $\mathrm{d}V_1$ in the y and z directions and add (vectorially) the three equations. Next, we observe that the molecules in $\mathrm{d}V_1$, $\mathrm{d}V_2$ and $\mathrm{d}V_3$ form a triangle whose sides, r_{23} and r_{31}, can be related to r_{12} by the cosine rule. Finally, the three pair distribution functions and the pair potentials are functions only of the distance between corresponding volume elements and so the pair distribution functions can all be expressed in terms of the radial distribution function. We need not write down the rather complex final equation which results from these manipulations, as its essential feature can be inferred from 8.17. This feature is that the unknown $\rho(r)$ appears both under an integral sign and in other terms outside it, giving an equation known as the Born, Green, Yvon or B.G.Y. integral equation.

Kirkwood, by a rather different approach, also obtained[4] an integral equation for $\rho(r)$. Up to the point in his analysis where the superposition approximation was inserted his procedure is different from, but equivalent to, the B.G.Y. method. Because the superposition approximation is not exact, however, the final form of Kirkwood's equation differs from that of the B.G.Y. equation in minor detail.

There are various techniques available for the solution of these integral equations, most of which involve the principle of successive approximation or iteration. That is, an approximate expression for $\rho(r)$, obtained by guesswork supplemented by knowledge of the correct limiting forms of $\rho(r)$ for small and large r, is substituted under the integral sign, but not elsewhere. The integral can then be evaluated, by numerical methods if necessary, giving a non-integral equation for $\rho(r)$, which can be solved. The new expression for $\rho(r)$ will, it is hoped, be a better approximation to the exact solution than the original guess. The whole process is then repeated by substituting this improved expression for $\rho(r)$ under the integral sign. By this process of iteration a series of approximations to the exact solution is obtained which, with luck and skill, will converge reasonably quickly. The procedure is tedious and it is sometimes necessary to make further approximations, but the use of computers makes it feasible.

Kirkwood and his collaborators[5] obtained solutions of the B.G.Y. equation for the cases of (a) hard non-attracting spheres, (b) the L.J. potential with a hard sphere 'cut off' near the origin and finally (c) the unmodified L.J. potential. The calculated $\rho(r)$ for all these cases reproduced the broad features of the diffraction data, a high first maximum followed by a number of smaller oscillations. For cases (b) and (c) the equation of state was worked out, using 8.3. The isothermals proved to exhibit the sinuous form below a certain temperature and a monotonic one above, so that the critical point could be identified. The critical data in molecular reduced units for case (c) are shown in the following table. They show reasonable agreement with experiment. However, at higher densities and low temperatures, in the liquid

TABLE 8.1

	p^*	V^*	T^*	RT/pV
Calc.	0·147	2·89	1·48	3·48
Exp.	0·116	3·14	1·25	3·44

region, some of the calculated pressures were negative, illustrating again the great sensitivity of the equation of state to the exact form of $\rho(r)$.

Recently, Broyles[6] has also solved the B.G.Y. equation for the

L.J. 6–12 potential. The calculations were made for the same reduced temperature $T^* = 2.74$ employed by Wood and Parker in their Monte Carlo work. Solutions were obtained for four reduced volumes $V^* = 2.5$, 1.2, 1.0 and 0.9, which lie within the Monte Carlo range, so that the results of the two methods could be compared. At the lower densities the results are in good agreement which progressively worsens as the density increases. The calculated radial distribution function for $V^* = 1.0$ is shown in fig. 8.1.

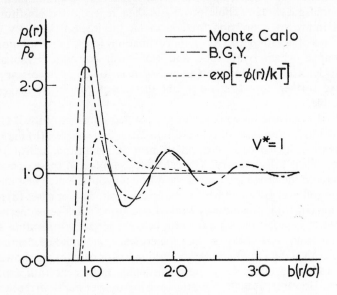

Fig. 8.1   The radial distribution function for a L.J. 6–12 fluid at $T^* = 2.74$ $V^* = 1$. For the Monte Carlo data $b = 1$. For the B.G.Y. data $b = 0.898$. The curve $\exp(-\phi(r)/kT)$ (for $b = 1$) is also shown

Broyles found that the B.G.Y. calculations did not agree with the Monte Carlo results, though if the abscissa of the B.G.Y. solution was adjusted by a scale factor of 0.898 the solutions could be made to agree at large distances. The important first peak, however, is not in agreement. Also shown in the figure is the curve obtained from $\rho(r) = \rho_0 \exp(-\beta\phi(r))$ which is the limiting form for $\rho(r)$ at very small and very large distances.

For the highest density studied by Broyles, $V^* = 0.9$, the distribution function is shown in fig. 8.2, together with the curve obtained from the Percus–Yevick integral equation (p. 136). This density is near to that corresponding to the discontinuity in the Monte Carlo calculations which is believed to indicate the gas–solid transition. It is of interest that Broyles was able to obtain a solution here, as it is generally supposed that solution procedure for the B.G.Y. must fail to converge in the neighbourhood of the transition. The agreement at this higher density is seen to be poor even at large distances.

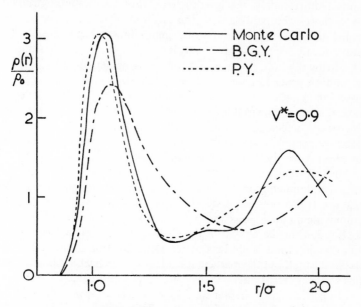

Fig. 8.2   The radial distribution function for a L.J. 6–12 fluid at $T^* = 2.74$ $V^* = 0.9$, according to three theories

The pressure and internal energy calculated from the B.G.Y. equation are shown in figs. 7.3 and 7.4. At low densities these are in essential agreement with the Monte Carlo results and the experimental data of Michels, but at the higher densities the agreement is again very poor.

In contrast to some of the earlier work of Kirkwood and his collaborators, Broyles' method of solution involved no serious approximations other than the use of the superposition approximation. The error in the calculated radial distribution function, due to the failure to iterate an infinite number of times, was probably less than 1%, except for the range between the origin and the point where the curve crosses the line $\rho(r)/\rho_0 = 1$ for the first time. The failure of the B.G.Y. equation to yield correct results at high densities must then be attributed squarely to the use of the superposition approximation. It has long been known that this approximation is unsatisfactory at high densities for those configurations of the three molecules which are intermediate between very close mutual separations and very distant ones. Unfortunately, this intermediate range, corresponding roughly to distances comparable with the position of the first peak in the radial distribution function, is of primary importance in liquids. It is also difficult to estimate how badly it does fail. A clue can be obtained by solving the B.G.Y. equation for gases at moderate densities where a solution procedure can be used which involves expansion of the equation in a series of powers of ρ_0, i.e. N/V. This leads to the equation of state in the virial form. It is then possible to compare the first few virial coefficients with the exact values from Mayer's cluster expansion method. The second and third virial coefficients are found to be given correctly, but not the higher coefficients.

Thus, further progress by the pair distribution method requires the abandonment, or modification, of the superposition approximation. It has been suggested by Cole[7] that this might be done by employing an analogous approximation for the quadruplet function $n_4(1, 2, 3, 4)$ in the second of the chain of linked integral equations, so obtaining what might be a better approximation for $n_3(1, 2, 3)$ for use in the first, but the mathematical labour which would be involved has so far deterred anyone from attempting this task.

For use in a later chapter we introduce here a convenient quantity, the potential of average force, $\psi(r)$. This may be defined by the equation

$$\rho(r) = \rho_0 \exp\left(-\beta . \psi(r)\right) \qquad 8.18$$

so that a knowledge of $\rho(r)$ is equivalent to a knowledge of $\psi(r)$. The physical meaning of $\psi(r)$ is that it is the effective mutual potential energy of a pair of molecules in a fluid after allowing for their interaction with the remaining $N-2$ molecules, and its negative gradient, $-\partial\psi(r)/\partial r$ gives the average force exerted by one molecule on the other under the same conditions. At very small r, $\psi(r)$ approaches $\phi(r)$, and at large r it approaches zero, in between it oscillates because of the corresponding oscillations in $\rho(r)$, $\psi(r)$ being large when $\rho(r)$ is small.

The method of collective variables

In recent years a radically different theory of fluids has been put forward which is known as the method of collective variables. As applied to liquids by Percus and Yevick[8] this new approach again yields an integral equation for the radial distribution function and so will be outlined briefly at this point.

We recall that the fundamental difficulty in the calculation of the partition function is due to the intractable nature of the integrations over the molecular coordinates in the configuration integral (p. 93). This difficulty arises because any one molecule is in strong interaction with many others, so that that part of the Hamiltonian function which represents the potential energy of the molecules cannot be separated into parts which depend on the coordinates of individual molecules only. The method of collective variables is a way of transforming the Hamiltonian so that this separation can be approximately realised.

Suppose we imagine the space occupied by a fluid divided into small volume elements by imaginary partitions, say cubical boxes whose sides are a few Ångstrom units in length. The number of molecules in any box will then fluctuate in time about a mean value as the molecules move about. Because of the intermolecular forces the fluctuations in any one box will influence those in adjacent boxes so that density variations will tend to be propagated through the fluid, at any rate over short distances. (Our simple cell theories take no account of these correlated fluctuations and the neglect of them leads to the communal errors.)

Now the propagation of density fluctuations is nothing more than the familiar phenomenon of the transmission of a sound wave. A sound wave consists of an alternation of compressions and rarefactions travelling through the medium, the molecular number–density in a compression exceeding the average and in a rarefaction falling below. This suggests that we may be able to interpret the microscopic fluctuations in fluids in terms of acoustic waves, constantly traversing the fluid in all directions. These waves are not generated by any agent external to the fluid, they are simply a different way of representing the unceasing molecular motion. Of course, a single simple harmonic wave would not be an adequate representation, this would correspond to a regular long-range variation in the number–density which would imply a degree of long-range order not present in fluids. We must think in terms of a very large number of waves of different wavelengths and the random microscopic density fluctuations in a fluid are then the result of the addition, or superposition, of all these waves.

A simple example of the superposition of standing waves is the motion of an elastic string fixed at the points $x=0$ and $x=L$. If set into vibration the displacement at any point may, in general, vary with x in a very complex manner. No matter how complex this variation, however, it can be described by the superposition of a large (possibly infinite) number of simple harmonic waves. This is the familiar procedure of Fourier synthesis. The allowed wavelengths of the Fourier components are determined by the conditions that the displacement must vanish at $x=0$ and $x=L$. This restricts the allowed frequencies to harmonics of the fundamental frequency and the allowed waves are of the form $\sin 2\pi x/\lambda$ with $\lambda=2L/n$. Here n is restricted to integral values by the boundary conditions.

We may translate this analogy into the collective variable description of a fluid. To this end let us consider a system of N particles constrained so that they can move only in one dimension in a limited region extending along the straight line between $x=0$ and $x=L$. If, due to the action of the interparticle forces, these particles are found to execute small vibrations about points equally spaced along the line, we shall have a one-dimensional model of a crystalline solid, with a lattice spacing of N/L. A one-dimensional model of a fluid would correspond to an absence of such long-range order, and the number of particles per unit length will then fluctuate around the mean value N/L.

In the ordinary statistical mechanical theory of such a one-dimensional fluid we would describe the instantaneous configuration in terms of the particle coordinates, $x_1 \ldots x_N$. In the method of collective variables new coordinates are introduced, the collective coordinates, each of which depends on all the x's. For our purposes we may take the first of these, q_1, to be defined by

$$q_1 = \sum_{i=1}^{N} \sin 2\pi x_i/\lambda_1 \qquad\qquad 8.19$$

The wavelength, λ_1, in this sum is that of one of the waves with which the acoustic-wave description of the system is to be built up. The general collective coordinate, q_n, is defined as

$$q_n = \sum_{i=1}^{N} \sin 2\pi x_i / \lambda_n \qquad 8.20$$

These collective coordinates are, effectively, Fourier components of the particle density.

To describe any configuration by the usual method we need just N coordinates, x_1 to x_N. Hence, in the new method we should have sufficient information if we take N collective coordinates, q_1 to q_N, and, in fact, difficulties and ambiguities arise if this number is exceeded.

To determine the allowed wavelengths, the same boundary conditions as for the elastic string can be applied, that is, $\lambda_n = 2L/n$, where n can take integral values from 1 to N. The shortest wavelength will then be $2L/N$, comparable with the average distance between particles. For a real three-dimensional fluid we require $3N$ collective coordinates whose associated wavelengths may be determined in a similar manner by supposing the fluid to be confined to a cube of side L.

The next stage is to reformulate the Hamiltonian function so that it becomes a function of the collective coordinates rather than the original Cartesian coordinates. The most difficult part of this is the transformation of the potential energy, Φ. For fluids it proves to be rather troublesome to obtain a sufficiently accurate representation of, say, the L.J. 6–12 potential with the limited allowed number of collective variables. The difficulty is connected with the fact that the minimum allowed wavelength is $2L/N$, while the L.J. 6–12 potential varies rapidly over distances comparable with this wavelength. The transformation involves complex mathematical procedures into which we shall not enter and whose justification is still open to question. On making the best transformation possible, however, the advantage of the collective variable method is revealed. The major part of the Hamiltonian proves to be separable into a sum of parts, each of which depends on only one of the collective variables. The way is therefore opened to the calculation of thermodynamic properties.

The collective variable method was originally applied, by Bohm and Pines,[9] not to liquids, but to such problems as the interaction of charged particles in ionised gases. In such a gas (a plasma) the density fluctuations appear as *plasma oscillations*, the coupled and synchronous motion of large numbers of charged particles. The electrostatic potential energy of a pair of charged particles varies rather slowly with their separation—as the inverse first power—so that density fluctuations are correlated over large distances. In liquids the potential energy varies much more rapidly—approximately as the inverse sixth power at large distances—and the application of the collective variable method is more difficult. Nevertheless, Percus and Yevick, in 1958, applied the method to molecular fluids and, after a lengthy analysis, were able to formulate an integral equation, the P.Y. equation, for the radial distribution function. This integral equation is very different from the integral equations of Born, Green and Yvon and Kirkwood.

The solution of the P.Y. integral equation has been obtained by Broyles for the same conditions as were used for the B.G.Y. equation. The radial distribution function and thermodynamic properties are shown in figs. 7.3, 7.4 and 8.2. It will be seen that it constitutes a great improvement on the B.G.Y. equation. The first peak in the radial distribution function (fig. 8.2) is in very good agreement with the Monte Carlo calculations. The agreement is less satisfactory at larger distances, though still better than the B.G.Y. equation. The P.Y. pressures (fig. 7.3) are in excellent agreement with the Monte Carlo results over the whole density range studied and pass about mid-way through the discontinuity near $V^* = 0.9$. The configurational internal energy is also in much better agreement (fig. 7.4).

There seems little doubt that the collective variable approach constitutes a significant advance in the theory of fluids at high densities. Final judgment must be deferred until more numerical calculations have been made and compared with experimental data. On general grounds one would expect this method to be of less value at low densities; in a dilute gas, for example, the molecular interactions are restricted to binary collisions and the concept of correlated fluctuations of density involving several molecules at a time becomes implausible. However, at low densities, other methods of adequate accuracy are available.

Studies on models

The attempts to calculate the radial distribution function described above have involved complex mathematical procedures and the numerical work requires an extensive use of electronic computers. It is of interest, therefore, that a great deal of illuminating information about the structure of liquids can be obtained from very simple experiments using apparatus available to any student of physics. In these experiments molecules are represented by solid balls and the experiments are undertaken to see how these balls can be packed together in a random manner. A number of experiments on such models have been made from time to time, most recently by Scott in Canada, and Bernal and his collaborators in England.

In Scott's preliminary experiments[10] a number of $\frac{1}{8}$ in. diameter steel ball-bearings were poured into an ordinary 100 ml measuring cylinder, sufficient to fill it to the 54·(5) ml level. On gently shaking and tapping, the level fell to 53·(0) ml. Further experiments showed that the random packing could be classified into two well-defined types; loose random packing, which is obtained when the balls fill the vessel by rolling down an existing heap of balls, and dense random packing which is obtained by shaking and tapping the vessel. For each type a packing density D can be defined as

$$D = \frac{\text{Total Volume of } N \text{ balls}}{\text{Volume of container occupied by } N \text{ balls}} = \frac{\frac{4}{3}\pi(\sigma/2)^3 N}{V}$$

8.21

where σ is the ball diameter.

To obtain proper estimates of packing densities it is necessary to correct for surface errors which arise because the dimensions of the container are not infinitely large compared with the ball diameter. The smooth inner surface also imposes a certain regularity in the geometrical arrangement of the balls in contact with it. In a second series of experiments a number of spherical flasks of different radii, R, were filled with the balls. The inner surfaces of these flasks were impressed with an irregular pattern of dimples and the largest could contain some 5000 balls. The number of balls in a flask could be obtained by weighing and the volume occupied by filling the empty flask with water to the same level as the balls. From these data the packing density, $D(R)$, for a flask of radius R was found. Scott argued that the error in D is proportional to (surface area/volume), that is to $1/R$, or very nearly to $(1/N^{\frac{1}{3}})$. A graph of $D(R)$ against $(1/N^{\frac{1}{3}})$ was indeed found to give a straight line which on extrapolation to $(1/N^{\frac{1}{3}})=0$ gave the true packing density, D.

In a final series of experiments a number of dimpled copper cylinders of different radii, R, were used, to give easier control of the packing. By filling one cylinder to different heights, h, plotting packing density against $1/h$ and extrapolating to $1/h=0$ one may correct for the finite height. Then, by taking these values for the different cylinders, plotting against $1/R$ and extrapolating to $1/R=0$, one may correct for the finite radius.

The experiments with the spherical flasks gave extrapolated values for D of 0·63(4) for dense random packing, and 0·59(1) for loose random packing, those with the cylinders 0·63(7) and 0·60(1), in essential agreement.

The interest of the figure for dense random packing is brought out by comparing it with the packing density for crystalline close-packed lattice structures. For f.c.c. and h.c.p. lattices of spheres the volume, V, occupied by N spheres is $N\sigma^3/\sqrt{2}$ (table 3.1) whence, from 8.21, the packing density is $\pi/3\sqrt{2}=0\cdot7405$. The ratio of crystalline to random dense packing is therefore 0·7405/0·637 or 1·16(3). The obvious comparison is with the density ratios of solid to liquid for the inert gases at their melting points. These are: Ne=1·15(8), A=1.15(2), Kr=1·15(8), Xe=1·14(8). Within the limits of experimental error the ratio is the same for the ball-bearings and the inert gases.

In a further experiment the radial distribution function for the balls was obtained. About 4000 balls were poured into a dimpled cylinder which could be separated into two halves. After shaking down to give dense random packing, molten paraffin wax was poured in and allowed to set. One-half of the cylinder was then taken off and the surface layer of exposed balls removed and disregarded. The three-dimensional Cartesian coordinates of each remaining ball were measured by scraping off the surface wax and reflecting light from the polished surface of a ball into a travelling microscope fitted with two horizontal scales and one vertical scale. After each ball was measured its surrounding wax was scraped away and the ball removed. By a painstaking series of measurements the coordinates of 1000 balls, referred to an arbitrary origin, were, in this way, determined to an accuracy of the order of 0·01 mm.

To determine the radial distribution function one ball was chosen at random as a new origin and the coordinates of all other balls referred to it. This was repeated for a number of other balls chosen as the origin (25 in all), and the results averaged to smooth out local variations in the surroundings of any one ball. From these data the average number of balls, N_{av}, at radial distances from the origin lying between r and $r+\Delta r$ was found, the successive intervals Δr being taken as one-fifth of the ball diameter. On division of these numbers by $4\pi r^2$ Scott obtained a quantity which is, effectively, the radial distribution function $\rho(r)$ for the balls. As an estimate of the reliability of the data the standard deviation was also calculated for each interval.

The distribution function so obtained is shown in fig. 8.3.

At 'large' distances, beyond some 4 ball diameters, $N_{av}/4\pi r^2$ approaches a steady value which agrees with that calculated from

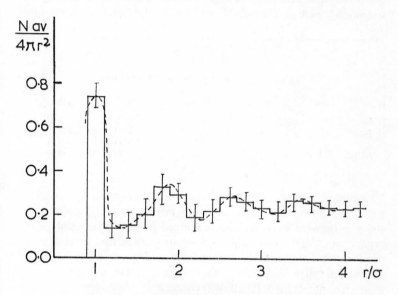

Fig. 8.3   The radial distribution of ball-bearings for dense random packing. The standard deviation of each observation is shown

dense random packing. The relative spacing of the peaks along the r-axis, taking the first peak as at unit distance, is compared with the neutron diffraction data of Henshaw[11] for the liquid inert gases near their melting points in table 8.2. Again, the agreement is seen to be remarkable.

The significance of the figure for loose random packing, if any, is, as yet, in doubt. From experiments on the shearing of a mass of balls, Scott[12] believes there may be some relationship of the figure to the phenomenon of viscous flow in simple liquids.

Bernal's experiments[13] were designed, primarily, to determine the coordination number, that is, the mean number of balls which touch, or very nearly touch, any arbitrary ball. Several thousand $\frac{1}{4}$-in. ball-bearings were poured into a rubber balloon, well shaken down and compressed by binding the mass together (the flexible rubber mini-mises the surface packing errors). The balls were soaked in black japan paint and set aside to dry. When unwrapped, a mass of adherent balls, resembling caviare, was obtained. By separating and examining the balls the number of 'actual' and 'near' contacts could

TABLE 8.2

Relative spacing of peaks in $\rho(r) - r$ curves

	1st	2nd	3rd	4th
He	1	1·8(7)	2·6(6)	3·5(8)
Ne	1	1·8(5)	2·7(7)	3·5(7)
A	1	1·8(1)	2·6(4)	3·4(4)
Balls	1	1·8(3)	2·6(4)	3·4(5)

be counted. Actual contact of two balls is revealed by unstained spots on their surfaces, near contact by raised mounds of paint where the gap between balls had been bridged by solidified paint before separation. Careful separate experiments showed that these mounds are formed if the distance between the centres of spheres does not exceed the sphere diameter by more than 5%. The numbers of both kinds of contacts for 500 balls was counted.

For this data the probability of finding n balls in actual or near contact with a central ball could be determined. The minimum number of actual contacts is four, since any ball must rest on three others and will support at least one. The maximum is twelve, but this number is highly improbable, and the distribution between these limits is somewhat skew. The mean number of contacts of both kinds was 8·5, of which 6·5 are actual contacts.

The importance of these coordination numbers is that the poten-tial energy of a liquid is determined largely by the nearest neighbours of a central molecule. The number of neighbours lying just beyond the limit for near contact is not revealed by the experiments and these would contribute appreciably to the potential energy. Scott's experi-ments showed that the number which lie between $1·0\sigma$ and $1·2\sigma$ is

9·3 ± 0·8. Estimates from the area of the first peak in neutron diffraction studies on the inert gases give 8·0 to 9·7.

The distance of closest approach of hard spheres is the same in crystalline and random packing, being equal to the sphere diameter. Bernal's experiments show that the greater specific volume of a liquid, compared with the solid, is to be attributed largely to a decrease in coordination number, from 12 in the solid to a value in the region of 8 to 10 in the liquid, while the most probable nearest-neighbour distance is little changed. This is also indicated by the diffraction data; the position of the first peak in the $\rho(r)$ curves varies little with temperature over most of the liquid range and differs little from the nearest-neighbour distance in the crystal.

The conclusion to be drawn from these experiments would appear to be that while, strictly, the structure of liquids is determined by thermodynamical criteria yet, nevertheless, this is to a large extent equivalent to a structure determined by geometrical factors. The importance of geometrical factors has been emphasised particularly by Bernal.[14] In his view pure mathematicians could greatly assist the study of the liquid state by developing the at present virtually non-existent science of *statistical solid geometry*, that is, the study of how non-regular geometrical solids can be packed together to occupy space as densely as possible.

9

THE TRANSPORT PROPERTIES

(1) THE MOLECULAR THEORY OF VISCOSITY

We have, so far, considered only those properties of fluids which are related to states of thermodynamic equilibrium. Such equilibrium is characterised by the uniformity of certain properties throughout the volume of the system and by the fact that these properties remain unchanged in time, except, perhaps, for minute fluctuations about a mean wholly beyond the limits of observation. In particular, we have supposed that the temperature everywhere within our system is uniform and unchanging and also that the fluid has no bulk motion, that is, it does not flow from one part of the system to another.

When we come to consider phenomena like thermal conduction, or viscous flow, we see that these phenomena relate essentially to fluids which are not in states of thermodynamic equilibrium. To observe thermal conduction we must establish a gradient of temperature within the fluid, and we then observe that heat energy is transported from the hotter to the colder parts. Similarly, viscous forces only appear when adjacent parts of a fluid are moving with different velocities, that is, when there exists a gradient of velocity. These forces, due to what Newton called a lack of slipperiness of the fluid, are of a frictional nature and tend to slow down the faster moving parts and speed up the slower moving parts. In this case there is a transport of momentum within the system. Thermal conduction and viscous flow are therefore called transport processes, and the coefficients of thermal conductivity and of shear viscosity are the transport coefficients. They are the constants of proportionality which relate the rates of flow of heat and momentum to the respective gradients of temperature and velocity.

We must expect that, at the molecular level, the transport properties of fluids, like the thermodynamic properties, are determined by the properties of the molecules; by their masses and by the intermolecular law of force. For the thermodynamic properties the link between the molecular picture and the macroscopic picture is provided by the laws of statistical mechanics, which we have employed in the form of Gibbs' canonical ensemble. For systems not in equilibrium, however, we cannot use this method. We therefore are confronted with two distinct problems. The first is to see how, at the molecular level, the flow of energy or momentum is related to the properties of the molecules. The second is to devise a statistical averaging procedure appropriate to systems which are not in equilibrium and so enable us to pass from the molecular picture to the

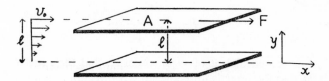

Fig. 9.1   The laminar flow of a fluid between a moving upper plate and a fixed lower plate

macroscopic picture. The first of these tasks proves to be much simpler than the second which, for liquids, involves difficulties which have not yet been fully overcome.

To illustrate the nature of the problems encountered in the theory of transport properties we shall select viscosity, a property which for many years has attracted attention from theoretical and experimental investigators. Much of the basic theory which is required to understand viscosity, however, applies also to the related phenomenon of thermal conductivity.

To define the coefficient of viscosity let us consider the experimental arrangement depicted in fig. 9.1. The space between two large parallel flat plates of area A, a distance l apart, is filled with fluid. The upper plate is dragged with constant velocity $\mathcal{V}_0$ to the right (x-direction) while the lower plate is fixed. It is found that fluids in such a situation can be divided into two groups. For gases and many ordinary liquids the external force, F, which must be applied to the upper plate to maintain a constant velocity is found to be strictly proportional to the velocity. Such fluids are called Newtonian fluids. For some liquids, however, the force is not proportional to the velocity, usually increasing less rapidly than the velocity, and these are called non-Newtonian liquids. Non-Newtonian behaviour is often exhibited by very viscous liquids whose molecules are very large or very long, but all common liquids with relatively small molecules are Newtonian fluids and we shall consider only these. For such fluids a natural supposition, confirmed by experiment, is that the x-component of velocity of the fluid between the plates varies linearly with distance, measured in the vertical (y) direction, from zero at the lower plate to $\mathcal{V}_0$ at the upper plate. The fluid is then in a condition of *steady laminar flow*, characterised by a velocity gradient $\mathcal{V}_0/l$. The force per unit area on the upper plate is related to this velocity by the equation

$$\frac{F}{A} = -\eta\,\frac{\mathcal{V}_0}{l} \qquad\qquad 9.1$$

where η is the coefficient of shear viscosity, and the negative sign indicates that the force is in the negative x-direction. Laminar flow, therefore, is associated with two mutually perpendicular directions in space, the direction of $\mathcal{V}_0$ (x-direction) and the direction of l (y-direction). To keep these two directions in mind we re-write equation 9.1 in the form

$$P_{xy} = -\eta G_{xy} \qquad\qquad 9.2$$

where $P_{xy}=F/A$ and $G_{xy}=\mathcal{V}_0/l$. Here P_{xy} is the tangential, or shear, stress exerted on the plate by the fluid. The first suffix indicates the direction of the shear stress and the second the direction of the axis normal to the plane of the plate. G_{xy} is the velocity gradient, whose directional properties are similarly indicated by the suffixes, the x-component of velocity varying in the y-direction.

In practice, there are more convenient methods of measuring η than the arrangement depicted in fig. 9.1. For simple fluids one usually determines η by measuring the rate of flow of the fluid through a capillary tube of known dimensions under a known pressure difference. The laws governing the rate of flow were extensively investigated by the physician Poiseuille in 1846, after whom the c.g.s. unit of viscosity, the poise, is named. These methods are described in most text-books on the properties of matter.

From the mass of experimental data on viscosity we may briefly summarise the main features as follows. The viscosity of simple non-polar liquids near the melting point is usually of the order of one hundredth of a poise and decreases rapidly with increasing temperature. Innumerable empirical equations have been proposed[1] to represent this variation, none of which will fit all liquids over a wide range. The viscosity of many simple liquids is, however, quite closely represented by the formula

$$\eta = A \exp (b/T) \qquad\qquad 9.3$$

where A and b are constants. It is understood that the formula refers to viscosities measured at constant (usually atmospheric) pressure. The effect of an increase in pressure is to raise the viscosity (water below about 20°C is anomalous).

As an increase in temperature reduces the density of a liquid while an increase in pressure raises it one is tempted to suppose that viscosity is a function only of the density, so that if the temperature and pressure were simultaneously varied so as to keep the density constant the viscosity would also remain constant. This has indeed been suggested but the extensive high pressure measurements of Bridgman have shown that it is not true in general. If kept at constant density the viscosity of liquids continues to fall with increasing temperature, though usually much less rapidly than at constant pressure. Much of Bridgman's work, however, was on liquids with fairly complicated molecules and the experimental data for monatomic liquids is not extensive. Recent measurements of the viscosity of liquid argon at constant density[2] show that the variation with temperature is very small, though if measured at constant pressure eq. 9.3 is well obeyed. The point is of importance because theories of viscosity are often based on an assumption of constant density.

Viscosity and momentum transport

We may link the molecular theory of viscous flow to the macroscopic theory by means of the fundamental law of dynamics, Newton's second law of motion, that the time rate of change of the momentum of a body is equal to the force acting upon it. Let F denote the force and δP the increment in momentum in time δt, then we may write, quite generally,

$$\delta P = F.\delta t \qquad\qquad 9.4$$

Let us first apply this equation to matter in bulk, that is, to the volume, V, of fluid between the parallel plates of fig. 9.1. We may interpret this figure as follows. The force acting on the upper plate is $F = P_{xy}.A$. In the interval δt this will impart to the fluid in contact with it a horizontal, or x-component, of momentum numerically equal to $F.\delta t$, or $P_{xy}.A.\delta t$. The lower fixed plate experiences an equal but oppositely directed dragging force due to the fluid. In time δt this will rob the fluid adjacent to it of momentum, also equal to $P_{xy}.A.\delta t$. The overall effect, therefore, is as though momentum were transferred through the fluid from the upper to the lower plate, that is, through a distance l. The rate of flow is equal to the magnitude transferred times the velocity of flow, that is to $(P_{xy}.A.\delta t).(l/\delta t) = P_{xy}.A.l$. But Al is the volume, V, of fluid between the plates, so that we arrive at the result that momentum is flowing in the negative y-direction at a rate equal to the shear stress on the boundary surface times the volume of the fluid, that is,

$$\text{Momentum Flow in positive } y\text{-direction} = P_{xy}.V \qquad 9.5$$

P_{xy} being actually a negative quantity, so that the flow is downward.

Now let us pass to the molecular picture and see how this flow of momentum arises. As usual, we shall confine the discussion to fluids whose molecules interact with central additive forces.

In fig. 9.2 let i and j be any pair of molecules in a fluid. At some instant of time molecule j will have a certain momentum whose x and y components p_{jx} and p_{jy} are as shown, and will be subject to a force $F(r_{ij})$, due to molecule i, acting along the line of centres. We may now recognise two distinct ways in which momentum flow can occur. First, because of its motion, molecule j will, in a time δt, move a distance $(p_{jy}/m)\,\delta t$ in the y-direction. This molecule therefore transports its own x-component of momentum p_{jx} in the y-direction at a rate $p_{jx}(p_{jy}/m)\,\delta t \div \delta t = (p_{jx}.p_{jy})/m$. A similar expression applies to molecule i and to all the other molecules in the fluid. Adding these contributions we may write for this mode of transfer the expression $\sum_j (p_{jx}.p_{jy})/m$, the summation being taken over all the N molecules in volume V. This we may call the kinetic contribution to the momentum flow.

The second contribution arises from the molecular forces. Due to the action of these forces the resultant momentum of j is continually changing at a rate which, again by Newton's second law, is equal to the vector sum of all the forces acting on it. Consider only the x-components of these forces and further consider only that x-component, X_{ji}, which is due to molecule i. From fig. 9.2 this component is $F(r_{ij})$ cos α where α is the angle between r_{ij} and the x-direction. In time δt this force will contribute an increment of momentum, $F(r_{ij}).\cos \alpha. \delta t$ to molecule j. Similarly, molecule i will suffer a change in its x-component of momentum due to the molecule j. By Newton's third law

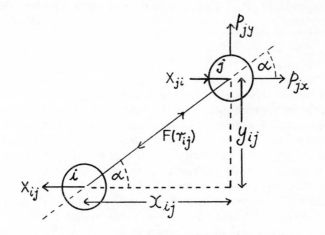

Fig. 9.2 The momentum transfer in a fluid arising from the motion and interaction of two molecules

these changes are equal in magnitude but opposite in direction and are such that if $F(r_{ij})$ is positive (repulsion) molecule j gains x-momentum while molecule i loses it. The net effect, therefore, is as though x-momentum equal to $F(r_{ij}) \cos \alpha. \delta t$ has been transferred, during δt, through space from molecule i to molecule j. Let the distance measured in the y-direction between molecules i and j, be y_{ij}, then the rate of transfer is $F(r_{ij}).\cos \alpha. \delta t.(y_{ij}/\delta t)=F(r_{ij}).\cos \alpha.y_{ij}$. Further, from fig. 9.2, $\cos \alpha=x_{ij}/r_{ij}$ so the rate of transfer is $F(r_{ij})(x_{ij}.y_{ij})/r_{ij}$. To evaluate the total flow we must sum this expression over all *pairs* of molecules in the volume V, i.e. $\sum_{\text{pairs}} F(r_{ij}) \times (x_{ij}.y_{ij})/r_{ij}$. This expression we may call the intermolecular force contribution to the momentum flow.

Adding both contributions we obtain, from 9.5,

$$P_{xy}V = \sum_j \frac{p_{jx} \cdot p_{jy}}{m} + \sum_{pairs} F(r_{ij}) \frac{x_{ij} \cdot y_{ij}}{r_{ij}} \qquad 9.6$$

This equation, which is applicable to both gases and liquids, expresses the momentum flow in terms of the molecular properties. Before examining it in more detail it is of interest to generalise our result to any kind of flow pattern, rather than the special case of laminar flow depicted in fig. 9.1. We may easily do this by writing down expressions corresponding to P_{xy} for all possible pairs of suffixes. We then obtain nine quantities which we may set out in an array, P, as follows

$$P = \begin{matrix} P_{xx} & P_{xy} & P_{xz} \\ P_{yx} & P_{yy} & P_{yz} \\ P_{zx} & P_{zy} & P_{zz} \end{matrix} \qquad 9.7$$

Each term in this array corresponds to an expression similar to 9.6 with the appropriate suffixes on the right-hand side.

This array has some interesting properties. First, we notice that interchanging x and y in 9.6 leaves the expression on the right-hand side unaltered, $P_{xy}=P_{yx}$ and similarly $P_{xz}=P_{zx}$; $P_{yz}=P_{zy}$, so that a flow of x-momentum in the y-direction is accompanied by an equal flow of y-momentum in the x-direction. Secondly, three of the terms, along a diagonal of the array, have similar suffixes, namely P_{xx}, P_{yy} and P_{zz}. The physical meaning of the first of these is that it represents the flow of x-component of momentum in the x-direction. Its value is obtained by setting y equal to x in 9.6 which gives

$$P_{xx} \cdot V = \sum_j \frac{p_{jx}^2}{m} + \sum_{pairs} F(r_{ij}) \frac{x_{ij}^2}{r_{ij}} \qquad 9.8$$

If we calculate the average value of the sum of the diagonal components we obtain

$$\frac{P_{xx}+P_{yy}+P_{zz}}{3}$$

$$= \frac{1}{V}\left\{ \frac{1}{3}\sum_j \frac{(p_{jx}^2+p_{jy}^2+p_{jz}^2)}{m} + \frac{1}{3}\sum_{pairs} F(r_{ij}) \frac{(x_{ij}^2+y_{ij}^2+z_{ij}^2)}{r_{ij}} \right\}$$

$$= \frac{1}{V}\left\{ \frac{1}{3}\sum_j \frac{p_j^2}{m} + \frac{1}{3}\sum_{pairs} F(r_{ij})r_{ij} \right\} \qquad 9.9$$

since, by Pythagoras, $p_j^2=p_{jx}^2+p_{jy}^2+p_{jz}^2$ and $r_{ij}^2=x_{ij}^2+y_{ij}^2+z_{ij}^2$.

The meaning of these manipulations becomes clear if we see what form our array takes for a fluid in thermodynamic equilibrium. There are then no velocity gradients, and therefore no direction in the fluid is distinguished from any other. Hence, in eq. 9.6, p_{jx} and p_{jy} are just as likely to be positive as negative, so that, when we sum over all molecules, the first term will average to zero. Similarly, x_{ij} and y_{ij} are equally likely to be positive or negative, so the second summation also vanishes. Thus P_{xy} and all the other non-diagonal terms in our array disappear. But this is only to be expected, because P_{xy} is a component of the shear stress on the surface bounding the fluid and in equilibrium this shear stress must be zero. The diagonal components, however, do not vanish, for the coordinates and momenta in 9.8 appear as squares and so are always positive. Our array therefore reduces to

$$P = \begin{matrix} P'_{xx} & 0 & 0 \\ 0 & P'_{yy} & 0 \\ 0 & 0 & P'_{zz} \end{matrix} \quad \text{(Equilibrium)} \qquad 9.10$$

where the primes indicate the equilibrium values of P_{xx}, etc. Furthermore, as there are no preferred directions, $P'_{xx}=P'_{yy}=P'_{zz}=p$, say. Equation 9.9 then has a simple and familiar interpretation, for p_j^2/m is just twice the kinetic energy of the jth molecule and we know from equilibrium theory that the sum of the kinetic energies of all the N molecules of a monatomic fluid has the value $\frac{3}{2}NkT$. So $\sum_j p_j^2/m$ is just $3NkT$ and eq. 9.9 becomes, on averaging

$$pV = NkT + \frac{1}{3}\overline{\sum_{\text{pairs}} F(r_{ij})r_{ij}} \qquad 9.11$$

If we identify p with the pressure, this is just Clausius' Virial Theorem (ch. 5, eq. 5.22). That each of the three diagonal components should be identified with the pressure follows quite naturally if we observe that, by our convention of suffixes, P_{xx} is the normal force per unit area on a bounding surface whose plane is itself normal to the x-direction.

The mathematical reader will guess that in the general array the nine quantities are the components of a symmetrical tensor† of the second order. A similar array, or tensor, G, can be set down for

† In a more formal treatment the components of P are, respectively, the normal (P_{xx} etc.) and shear (P_{xy} etc.) stresses exerted on the surfaces of an element $\delta x\, \delta y\, \delta z$ of fluid by the surrounding fluid.

the velocity gradient and the flow of viscous fluids can, in fact, be most concisely and elegantly described with the aid of the tensor calculus. We need not pursue this aspect of the subject further but it may be remarked in passing that, in a general flow pattern, it is necessary to distinguish rather carefully between the velocity gradient tensor G and the rate of strain tensor S. The components of these tensors are related by the rule $S_{xy} = (G_{xy} + G_{yx})/2$, etc. The coefficient of shear viscosity should then properly be defined as the coefficient which relates any off-diagonal component of P to twice the corresponding component of S, for example $P_{xy} = -2\eta S_{xy}$. For the special case of the laminar flow of fig. 9.1 the rate of strain S_{xy} is one-half of G_{xy}, in which case we recover the ordinary definition of η. We may avoid these complications and the use of the tensor calculus by confining ourselves to steady laminar flow, where the flow of momentum is given by 9.6.

Gases and liquids

Although eq. 9.6 applies equally to gases and liquids, the relative importance of the two contributions to the momentum flow differs greatly in the two cases. For gases, up to quite high pressures, the first term is by far the more important. A gas molecule can travel long distances (on a molecular scale) without coming close to a neighbour and so can transport its momentum very efficiently by the kinetic mechanism. If we adopt the simple hard-sphere model of a molecule, the intermolecular force vanishes except at the moment of a collision. The kinetic contribution can then be approximately evaluated very simply, by introducing the idea of the mean free path, λ, that is, the average distance travelled by a molecule between collisions. The flow of momentum is calculated by considering two parallel layers of streaming gas separated by a distance λ. Exchange of momentum between the layers is proportional to their relative velocity (that is, to the velocity gradient), to the density of the gas, ρ, and to the velocity, p_y/m with which the molecules cross from one layer to the other. This last is of the order of magnitude of the mean speed of the molecules, $\bar{c}$. Simple reasoning based on these ideas leads to the result

$$\eta = K.\rho\bar{c}\lambda \qquad 9.12$$

where K is a numerical constant of the order of unity. Further simple reasoning relates λ to the diameter, σ, of the sphere and gives

$$\lambda = \frac{K'm}{\rho\sigma^2} \qquad 9.13$$

where K' is again of the order of unity. The viscosity is therefore related to the molecular properties by

$$\eta = KK' \frac{m\bar{c}}{\sigma^2} \qquad\qquad 9.14$$

This formula predicts that viscosity should be independent of pressure and proportional to $\bar{c}$, that is, to the square root of the absolute temperature. The first of these predictions is well obeyed for gases over a wide range of pressure. The second is less well obeyed, a failure which can be attributed to the inadequacy of the hard-sphere model for the collision process.

This mean free path method of calculation is due to Maxwell. He and his successors went on to develop more rigorous theories and to allow for more realistic laws of intermolecular force. Modern methods of calculation[3] are due principally to Boltzmann, Enskog and Chapman, and by 1924 the theory was sufficiently exact to allow Lennard–Jones to deduce the parameters in the intermolecular force law from the measured viscosity coefficient. We may take it that the theory of gas viscosity is established on a satisfactory foundation, a foundation which depends on the fact that gas molecules are, for most of the time, out of the effective range of the intermolecular force of their neighbours.

For liquids this foundation cannot be used to erect a theory of viscosity. A molecule in a liquid is permanently subject to strong forces due to some dozen or so close neighbours and so the concept of a 'free' path is quite meaningless. Because its freedom of movement is so restricted it cannot transfer an appreciable amount of momentum by the kinetic mechanism and so the viscosity of a liquid is determined almost entirely by the second term in eq. 9.6. Our main task, therefore, is to find some way of evaluating the summation in the intermolecular force term for pairs of molecules in a liquid maintained in steady laminar flow.

In equilibrium theory we saw that such a summation could be given a clearer physical meaning by introducing the radial distribution function $\rho(r)$. This enabled us to relate Clausius' Virial Theorem to the equation of state of the fluid (ch. 8, eq. 8.3). An analogous procedure can be used to represent the expression for P_{xy}. In equilibrium the radial distribution function is spherically symmetrical, it is a function of r only. In laminar flow we cannot assume that this symmetry is maintained, we must expect that the radial distribution function will be distorted by the flow, the distortion increasing with the velocity gradient. We can easily generalise our definition of the radial distribution function so as to take account of this distortion, most conveniently with the aid of a spherical polar coordinate system. Let any molecule be chosen as the origin and consider a small volume element, δV, whose centre is at a distance r and whose direction is located by the angles θ and ϕ. Then the average number of molecules whose centres are to be found within δV will depend on r, θ and ϕ, and may be written $\rho(r, \theta, \phi) \cdot \delta V$. The function $\rho(r, \theta, \phi)$ is to be regarded as our generalised radial distribution function. Figure 9.3

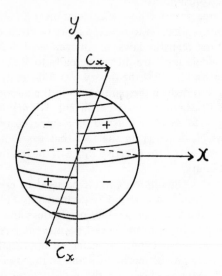

Fig. 9.3   The variation of number–density from the mean in laminar flow, near to an arbitrarily-chosen origin molecule

represents the distorted density distribution of molecules in a spherical region surrounding the central molecule. The number–density $\rho(r, \theta, \phi)$ exceeds the equilibrium value in the first and third quadrants and falls below it in the second and fourth, and the mean number of molecules within any volume element δV therefore depends both on its distance and direction from the origin.

When the velocity gradient is very small the distortion is also small, and in this case it can be shown from the spatial symmetry of the flow pattern that the distortion is zero in the x- and y-directions and a maximum or minimum at $45°$ to these directions.

To evaluate the expression $\sum_{\text{pairs}} F(r_{ij})(x_{ij}.y_{ij})/r_{ij}$ of eq. 9.6 we proceed as follows. Let molecule i be placed at the origin and consider the contribution made to the sum by the molecules in the volume element δV, whose coordinates relative to i are then all effectively equal to x, y, z. In spherical polars we have $x = r \sin \theta \cos \phi$; $y = r \sin \theta \sin \phi$; $z = r \cos \theta$ and $\delta V = r^2 \sin \theta \, d\theta \, d\phi \, dr$. The number of molecules in δV is $\rho(r, \theta, \phi) . \delta V$, so their contribution to the sum is

$$\rho(r, \theta, \phi) F(r) \frac{xy}{r} \, \delta V = F(r) . r^3 . \rho(r, \theta, \phi) \sin^3 \theta \sin \phi \cos \phi \, dr \, d\theta \, d\phi$$

We now integrate this expression over the volume of the liquid, repeat the process for each of the N molecules chosen in turn as the origin molecule and finally divide by two to correct for the counting of each pair twice. The momentum flow $P_{xy} V$ becomes, if we neglect the kinetic contribution as of little importance in liquids,

$$P_{xy} V = \frac{N}{2} \int F(r) r^3 \rho(r, \theta, \phi) \sin^3 \theta \sin \phi \cos \phi \, dr \, d\theta \, d\phi \qquad 9.15$$

where the single integral sign really represents three integrations over the variables r, θ and ϕ.

In equilibrium, when $\rho(r, \theta, \phi)$ becomes $\rho(r)$, the integration over the angles can be easily performed (θ ranges from 0 to π, ϕ from 0 to 2π) with the result that P_{xy} vanishes, as of course it ought to do. Thus the momentum flow can be interpreted as arising from the distortion of the radial distribution function.

There is, unfortunately, little hope of being able to investigate this distortion experimentally. In principle this might be done by X-ray or neutron diffraction experiments on liquids maintained in steady laminar flow, but it is likely that the small magnitude of the distortion even for the highest attainable velocity gradients is beyond the limits of detection.

When the velocity gradient is very small we may assume that the distortion is also very small, so that $\rho(r, \theta, \phi)$ will differ but little from $\rho(r)$. We may then assume that the distorted function can be represented by

$$\rho(r, \theta, \phi) = \rho(r)(1 + G_{xy} u(r) \sin^2 \theta \sin \phi \cos \phi) \qquad 9.16$$

where the second term in the bracket is small compared with unity.

6

This expression may be regarded as the expansion of $\rho(r, \theta, \phi)$ in a series of powers of the velocity gradient, terminating at the linear term. The angular dependence is of the correct symmetry, which is that of the product $x.y$ which occurs in the pair summation. The unknown function $u(r)$ represents the purely radial part of the distortion. When 9.16 is substituted in 9.15 the two terms in the bracket above give two integrals, of which the first vanishes for the reasons just discussed. The second gives

$$P_{xy} = \frac{N}{2V} G_{xy} \int F(r) . \rho(r) . u(r) r^3 \sin^5 \theta \sin^2 \phi \cos^2 \phi \, dr \, d\theta \, d\phi$$

$$9.17$$

The integrations over the angles can now be carried out and give a numerical factor of $4\pi/15$. Finally, on setting $P_{xy} = -\eta G_{xy}$ and introducing the intermolecular potential function $F(r) = -(d\phi(r)/dr)$ we obtain

$$\eta = \frac{2\pi}{15} \frac{N}{V} \int \frac{d\phi(r)}{dr} \cdot \rho(r) . u(r) r^3 \, dr \qquad 9.18$$

The quantity G_{xy} has disappeared from this equation, giving a viscosity coefficient independent of the velocity gradient. This is a necessary requirement if the liquid is to exhibit Newtonian viscosity and justifies the retention of only the linear term in 9.16.

In order to estimate numerical values of η we need to know $\phi(r)$, $\rho(r)$ and $u(r)$ as functions of r. About the first two we know a good deal, the intermolecular potential function $\phi(r)$ can be adequately represented by, say, the L.J. 6–12 potential and information about the equilibrium radial distribution $\rho(r)$ can be obtained from equilibrium theory and diffraction experiments. About $u(r)$ very little is known at the present time. Before we describe the attempts which have been made to calculate $u(r)$ let us, following H.S. Green,[4] try to make some qualitative deductions from eq. 9.18. First, we may be fairly confident that the most important contribution to the integral will come from a restricted range of the variable r, as we may see if we recall the general shapes of $\rho(r)$ and $\phi(r)$ as functions of r. For distances less than a molecular diameter, or say the σ of the 6–12 potential, $\rho(r)$ falls rapidly to zero—much more rapidly than $\phi(r)$ increases—so that the product $\rho(r) \, d\phi(r)/dr$ vanishes at small r. On the other hand, at distances greater than, say, 2σ or 3σ, $\rho(r)$ becomes effectively constant and equal to ρ_0, while $d\phi(r)/dr$ now goes rapidly to zero. Thus, unless $u(r)$ behaves in an unruly manner at small or large r, the integrand will only have a significant magnitude over a range of r extending from somewhat less than σ to 2σ or 3σ and so the viscosity of a liquid will be determined largely by the near neighbours of a molecule, as we might expect.

Can we now make some estimate of the effect of temperature on viscosity? $\phi(r)$ is, of course, independent of T and as a rough approximation we may take $\rho(r)$ as being proportional to $\exp(-\phi(r)/kT)$ where, in the important range of r, $\phi(r)$ is numerically negative (more accurately $\rho(r)$ is proportional to $\exp(-\psi(r)/kT)$ where $\psi(r)$ is the potential of average force, a quantity which may depend on T. Unless $u(r)$ is sharply temperature dependent then, we may guess that the exponential temperature-dependence is approximately retained after integration, giving a viscosity–temperature relation of the form $\eta \propto \exp b/T$ where b represents some average value of $-\phi(r)/k$ (or $-\psi(r)/k$) in the important range of r. In this way, according to H. S. Green, the approximate validity of eq. 9.3 is accounted for. In the absence of more detailed information about $\psi(r)$ and $u(r)$ this conclusion must, however, be regarded as very tentative.

Another interesting feature of the integral in eq. 9.18 is its close resemblance to the expression for the configurational contribution to the pressure in equilibrium theory (eq. 8.3). In fact, if $u(r)$ is replaced by a constant the two integrals are, apart from numerical constants, identical. When we recall the extreme sensitivity of the calculated pressure to the precise form of $\rho(r)$ we may guess that viscosity may also be sensitively dependent on $\rho(r)$ and therefore on the density. We begin to see why the temperature and pressure dependence of the viscosity of liquids is likely to be a very complex problem, not amenable to the simple kinds of arguments which work so well for gases.

Before we can make further progress we need to know more about the function $u(r)$. The calculation of $u(r)$ is related to the question of the behaviour of more general types of molecular distribution functions for fluids not in equilibrium, and is intimately connected with the problem of finding a proper statistical averaging procedure for such fluids. This, the second of the two problems mentioned at the beginning of this chapter, necessitates a return to more fundamental aspects of irreversible processes and to this question we now turn.

10

THE TRANSPORT PROPERTIES

(2) THE PROBLEM OF IRREVERSIBILITY

'By reason of the Tenacity of Fluids, and Attrition of their Parts. . . . Motion is much more apt to be lost than got, and is always upon the Decay.' NEWTON[1]

We have seen that to establish a molecular theory of viscosity we need to know the radial distribution function $\rho(r, \theta, \phi)$ for a fluid which is not in equilibrium. In equilibrium theory we derived the radial distribution $\rho(r)$ from the pair distribution n_2. The pair distribution was itself derived from the complete distribution function in coordinates and momenta of all the N molecules f_N, by appropriate integrations (pp. 86 ff.).

In non-equilibrium situations we may again formally set up a distribution, say $f_N(t)$, but $f_N(t)$ will not be the same as the equilibrium distribution and will vary with time. As a system approaches equilibrium $f_N(t)$ and the various reduced distribution functions obtainable from it will approach their equilibrium values. We are thus led to examine how our hierarchy of distribution functions vary with time.

At the outset of this task we encounter a curious paradox, the paradox of macroscopic irreversibility and microscopic reversibility. If, say, a stirred and unequally heated fluid is isolated, it will approach equilibrium as viscous forces and thermal conduction dissipate the bulk motion and even out the temperature gradients. Such changes always proceed in the same direction in time. It is never observed that fluids in equilibrium acquire, spontaneously, rotary motion or temperature gradients. In thermodynamics this one-way trend is expressed by the law of increase of entropy, which states that the entropy of an isolated system increases to a maximum at equilibrium and that, thereafter, spontaneous decreases in entropy are not observed.

At the molecular level it is difficult to see how this irreversibility arises. A collision between two gas molecules, for example, can be described by mathematical equations—the laws of conservation of energy and momentum—with which the magnitude and direction of the velocities after collision can be calculated from those before. The equations, however, apply equally well to the reversed molecular paths, there is nothing *in the equations themselves* which we can use to decide in which direction in time the collision process actually occurs. The same is true if we consider the equations which describe more complex interactions involving three, four or any number of molecules, whether in a gas or liquid. For N molecules this interaction can be described by the function $f_N(t)$ and it can be shown by setting up a formal equation for $f_N(t)$ (the Liouville Equation[2]; it is essentially a reformulation of Newton's laws of motion for the system of N molecules) that 'forward' and 'reversed' molecular motions are equally allowable. If, therefore, at the molecular level the motions are reversible in time, how are we to explain the irreversible trend to equilibrium always observed macroscopically?

In this form the paradox is known as Loschmidt's Reversibility Paradox. In another form it appears as Zermelo's Recurrence Paradox. This form is based on a theorem of the mathematician Poincaré which can be stated as follows: 'In a system of particles of finite total volume and energy and subject to forces which depend only on their spatial coordinates any given initial state must, in general, recur, not exactly but to any desired degree of accuracy infinitely often.' By a 'given initial state' is meant the specification of the numbers of particles to be found within the various small, but finite, elements of coordinate and momentum space. According to the theorem a fluid whose initial distribution function $f_N(t)$ describes a system in which there are observable temperature or velocity gradients will, if left isolated for an unlimited time, continually return to this state, and Zermelo therefore also argued that the laws of particle dynamics are incompatible with the thermodynamic principle of irreversible increase in entropy. The average time taken for a given initial state to recur is known as the period of the Poincaré cycle. It will depend, among other factors, on the number of particles in the system and on with what precision we choose to define the initial state, that is, on how small the elementary ranges of position and momentum are taken to be.

We shall not discuss in detail the attempts which have been made, by Boltzmann and others, to resolve these paradoxes. Roughly speaking, the explanation usually advanced[3] is as follows. The second law of thermodynamics—the principle of increase in entropy—does not tell us what *must* happen to a system but what will *very probably* happen. At equilibrium in any system the entropy does not remain absolutely constant at its maximum value. Tiny fluctuations of entropy occur quite frequently. At longer intervals somewhat greater fluctuations may occur. Once in a blue moon an absurdly small chance comes off and an even greater spontaneous decrease of entropy takes place which might correspond, say, to the appearance of perceptible bulk motion in a fluid system. The probability that this will happen is, however, so small that it may for practical purposes be entirely disregarded; we should probably have to wait for a time many times greater than the entire age of the universe to observe it. Thus, in this view, the apparent conflict between microscopic reversibility and macroscopic irreversibility simply arises because we can only observe a system over a limited period of time.

This resolution of the paradox does not, however, assist us in establishing a statistical procedure for handling irreversible processes. If we start with the dynamically reversible equations of motion of the molecules and build up to the macroscopic picture we must, at some point, insert into the theory an assumption which ensures that our final equations will describe the irreversible evolution to equilibrium always observed in practice and which cuts out the 'reversed' solutions. In all applications of theoretical physics to irreversible processes some such assumption is made, and there is a variety of ways in which this can be done. In each case the particular assumption made will be related to the averaging process needed to pass from the molecular to the macroscopic picture. As in all scientific theories the validity of the particular assumption made must ultimately be tested by comparison of theory with experiment.

As an example let us take the theory of the viscosity of dilute gases. For laminar flow the fundamental problem here is the evaluation of the sum $\sum_j p_{jx}p_{jy}/m$, which gives the dominating contribution to the momentum flow. The usual text-book treatment of viscosity, out-lined previously, is really an approximate way of evaluating this sum, based on Maxwell's mean free path concept, often combined with Joule's six-stream approximation for the velocity distribution function. The particular assumption which introduces the necessary irre-versibility is often concealed in the elementary treatment; it amounts to the assumption that a molecule crossing from one layer of stream-ing gas to the other will, on average, start with a mean x-component of velocity equal to that of the bulk motion of the first layer and, after a collision, will acquire a velocity equal to the bulk motion of the other layer. In the more rigorous theories the assumption takes the form of the Hypothesis of Molecular Chaos which, in one form, states that the momentum of a molecule after a small number of collisions is statistically independent, in magnitude and direction, of its original momentum. This assumption, as it were, frees the dyna-mical behaviour of the molecules from the reversibility implied in their equations of motion. The future evolution of the system then becomes a matter of probability rather than certainty and it is asserted that the observed irreversibility corresponds to the most probable evolution of the molecular distribution functions, when calculated with the aid of the above hypothesis.

We turn now to the problem of finding an assumption which will enable us to treat irreversible processes in liquids. In liquids the concept of collisions is not applicable, so the Hypothesis of Molecu-lar Chaos is not suitable for our purpose.

Kirkwood's hypothesis for liquids

In 1946 Kirkwood[4] put forward a general theory of irreversible processes in liquids. The assumption he made to secure the necessary irreversibility is concerned with the statistical properties of the force which acts on a representative molecule. The meaning of the assump-tion can be understood by recalling the nature of molecular motion in liquids.

As we know, a liquid molecule is permanently in strong interaction with some dozen or so neighbours, and the resultant force on it at some instant t, say $\mathbf{F}(t)$, will be the vector sum of the forces due (mainly) to these neighbours. As the molecular motion goes on this force will fluctuate rapidly in magnitude and direction and a short time later, say $t+s$, will have a different value, $\mathbf{F}(t+s)$. If we could solve the equations of motion for all the molecules we should be able to calculate $F(t+s)$ from $F(t)$ for any value of s. Instead of attempting this profitless task Kirkwood assumed that after a certain interval, τ the force on the molecule can be taken to be statistically independent of its earlier value. The magnitude of the interval τ can be expected to be a very small fraction of a second indeed. An important point is that it should be very much less than the duration of any experimental measurement made on the liquid.

In conventional statistics the term 'statistical independence' is given a precise mathematical measure by introducing a *correlation coefficient*. Kirkwood's hypothesis is similarly given a precise formulation, as follows. Form the scalar product of the vectors $F(t)$ and $F(t+s)$. This product may be positive or negative. Now calculate the average value, ξ, of the product over an equilibrium ensemble of systems, each containing a representative molecule similar to the one considered. Denoting a scalar product by a dot between the vectors and the ensemble average by a bar, the above procedure is represented by

$$\xi = \overline{F(t).F(t+s)} \qquad\qquad 10.1$$

Kirkwood's hypothesis is then

$$\xi \neq 0 \quad\text{if}\quad s < \tau; \qquad \xi = 0 \quad\text{if}\quad s > \tau$$

with the additional requirement that these conditions hold, no matter what the value of t.

Thus if the interval s is zero then 10.1 becomes $\overline{(F(t))^2}$, which is clearly positive. If, however, s is greater than τ then the sum in 10.1 will, according to the hypothesis, consist of terms which are just as likely to be positive as negative, and so the average will vanish. Speaking colloquially, one may say that a molecule after an interval τ is assumed to lose all 'memory' of the magnitude and direction of the force it experienced at the beginning of the interval. The expression ξ is called the auto-correlation function of the force $F(t)$.

The next step in Kirkwood's theory is to show that, for a moving molecule, the fluctuating force can be regarded as made up from the sum of two contributions. If our chosen molecule were at rest the fluctuating force would be completely random in direction. However, the molecule is never really at rest, like its neighbours it too is in continual motion. If, at some time, it has a velocity in a particular direction the fluctuations will no longer be quite random in direction and, on average, it is easy to see that they will tend to oppose the motion.

For example, if we could, by some means, shoot an argon atom at speed through liquid argon we would scarcely expect the initial velocity to be maintained, the projected atom would be rapidly slowed down by interaction with the other atoms. We may interpret this retarding effect as a kind of frictional force which comes into play when any atom is in motion. Kirkwood was able to show that it is probably a good approximation to take the frictional force as depending only on the velocity, $\mathbf{v}$, of the molecule and as being directly proportional to it, say $-\alpha\mathbf{v}$. Here α is a constant, the friction constant, which plays an important part in the whole theory.

We may therefore write

$$\mathbf{F}(t) = -\alpha\mathbf{v} + \mathbf{G}(t) \qquad\qquad 10.2$$

where $\mathbf{G}(t)$ now is a directionally random fluctuating force on a moving molecule which remains when the frictional force is subtracted from the total force $\mathbf{F}(t)$.

The equation of motion of our molecule is

$$m\frac{d\mathbf{v}}{dt} = \mathbf{F}(t) \qquad\qquad 10.3$$

or

$$m\frac{d\mathbf{v}}{dt} + \alpha\mathbf{v} = \mathbf{G}(t) \qquad\qquad 10.4$$

In reality, this representation of the asymmetric part of the force $\mathbf{F}(t)$ as a steady frictional drag on the molecule involves an averaging process which smooths the asymmetry. We would therefore expect there to be a relation between the statistical properties of $\mathbf{F}(t)$ and the friction constant α. The statistical properties of $\mathbf{F}(t)$ are embodied in the original assumption 10.1 and perhaps the most important result of Kirkwood's analysis is that he was able to deduce this relation. It is

$$\alpha = \frac{1}{3kT}\int_0^{\tau_1} \overline{\mathbf{F}(t).\mathbf{F}(t+s)}.ds \qquad\qquad 10.5$$

In this equation τ_1 is a second interval which must be chosen to be greater than τ. We recall that after the interval τ the integrand becomes zero, while for lesser times it does not vanish. Provided then that τ_1 is taken to be greater than τ the integral will reach a constant value, called a plateau value, and extension of the range of integration beyond τ_1 will not contribute anything further. One may ask why, in that case, the upper limit should not simply be put equal to infinity. Kirkwood, however, points out that to do so would lead to serious difficulties connected with the recurrence of the Poincaré cycle. We recall that the irreversible behaviour of a physical system is only apparent provided it is observed over times which are short compared with the period of the Poincaré cycle. If the integration were extended over an indefinitely great interval a fluctuation would occur which would cancel the original contribution and the integral would vanish. The upper limit τ_1, must therefore in principle be restricted, though it may be regarded as infinite for practical purposes.

Kirkwood's theory and Brownian motion

We have seen that the motion of a molecule in a liquid can be regarded as due to two opposing tendencies. It cannot remain at rest, for the fluctuating force will keep it in motion. On the other hand, as soon as it is in motion the frictional force comes into play to oppose the motion. Under the combined influence of these two the molecule will trace out a random zig-zag path which eventually causes it to drift away from its original position and wander in an irregular manner throughout the fluid.

Now a very similar type of behaviour can actually be observed in the phenomenon of the Brownian motion. When very small solid particles suspended in a fluid are viewed in a powerful microscope, they are seen to exhibit an irregular motion which, in time, causes them to wander away from their original position. This motion, first observed in pollen grains by the botanist Robert Brown in 1828, is now known to be a result of the random bombardment of the particles by the molecules of the fluid, an explanation apparently first suggested by Delsaux in 1877. The first conclusive demonstration that this is the correct explanation came in 1905 when Einstein succeeded in working out a quantitative theory of the phenomenon.

In Brownian motion the forces acting on a particle are analysed in a similar way to the above. The particle is kept in motion by the rapid bombardment of its surface by the molecules of the fluid, which may be represented by a fluctuating force $G(t)$, but in addition is subject to a frictional retarding force. Because a Brownian particle is so large compared with a molecule this frictional force can, for Brownian particles, be given a direct hydrodynamical interpretation. According to Stokes' Law the force on a spherical particle, of radius a, in a medium of viscosity η, is equal to $-6\pi\eta a\mathbf{v}$ and so is proportional to the velocity. Therefore, for a Brownian particle we can set up an equation exactly similar to 10.4. Indeed, we have here reversed the historical order of events, eq. 10.4 was originally formulated for Brownian motion, by Langevin[3] in 1906.

We may therefore regard Kirkwood's theory as an interpretation of molecular motion in terms of Brownian movement, in which the representative molecule is regarded as a Brownian particle. The chief point of difference is that, whereas in Brownian motion the friction constant α is equated to $6\pi\eta a$, in Kirkwood's theory this interpretation is not possible because Stokes' Law cannot be expected to apply to molecules. Information about the magnitude of the friction constant α is, therefore, to be obtained from 10.5.

Because of the close relationship of the two theories we shall make a short digression to illustrate the kinds of problems encountered in Brownian motion theory and see how their solutions are related to the theory of liquids. In the first place we note that the only kind of information we have about the fluctuating force is statistical information, and it follows that the only kind of prediction we can make about the behaviour of Brownian particles is in the nature of forecasts of probabilities, in particular of probability distribution functions.

Let us consider the following problem. A droplet of liquid containing a large number of particles is placed in the pure liquid at $t=0$. Neglecting gravitational or other external forces, what will be the future distribution of particles in space at some later time t? This was the problem first solved by Einstein[5] in 1905. He showed that the behaviour of the particles can be interpreted in two ways. At the microscopic level we may say that the Brownian motion causes the particles to wander away from their original position in random directions until they spread uniformly throughout the available volume. On the other hand, at the macroscopic level this spreading out of a collection of particles can be interpreted as a diffusion process, diffusion taking place from regions of high to regions of low concentration. In the diffusion interpretation the variation of the concentration, c, of particles is determined by the diffusion equation,

$$\frac{\partial c}{\partial t} = D\left\{\frac{\partial^2 c}{\partial x^2}+\frac{\partial^2 c}{\partial y^2}+\frac{\partial^2 c}{\partial z^2}\right\} = D\nabla^2 c \qquad 10.6$$

where D is the coefficient of diffusion. If these two ways of interpreting the spreading-out process are really only two different descriptions of the same phenomenon, there should be a connection between the friction constant α and the diffusion coefficient D. By using the statistical postulates of Brownian movement theory Einstein succeeded in deriving the diffusion equation and showed that the required relation is $D = kT/\alpha$.

The importance of this result is, first, that diffusion is an irreversible process, and, second, that the diffusion equation can usually be readily solved for given initial and boundary conditions to yield the concentration as a function of the coordinates and the time. Moreover, the concentration c can be interpreted as one of our hierarchy of distribution functions for, by its definition, $c\,\delta V$ gives the average number of particles to be found in a volume element δV and is therefore identical with our (now time-dependent) function $n_1\,\delta V$, the singlet distribution, except that it refers to Brownian particles rather than molecules. The solution of the equation will therefore tell us *how a time-dependent probability distribution function varies in an irreversible process.*

Following Einstein's pioneering research a number of investigators extended and generalised the theory so as to solve more difficult problems. In the above simple problem Einstein considered only the motion of a free particle, that is, one subject to no forces other than the fluctuating and frictional forces. More generally, let the particle also be subject to an external force, $\mathbf{K}$ (such as gravity), which may or may not depend on its coordinates. This force should now be added to the right-hand side of the Langevin equation 10.4. In this case Smoluchowski[6] showed that the corresponding generalisation of the diffusion equation is, in vector notation, and with c replaced by n_1

$$\frac{\partial n_1}{\partial t} = \text{div}\left(\frac{kT}{\alpha}\,\text{grad}\,n_1 - \frac{\mathbf{K}}{\alpha}\,n_1\right) \qquad 10.7$$

which is known as Smoluchowski's equation. If $\mathbf{K} = 0$ the right-hand side becomes $(kT/\alpha)\,\text{div grad}\,n_1 = (kT/\alpha)\nabla^2 n_1$ which, with $D = (kT/\alpha)$, reduces to the diffusion equation.

As an example of a case when $\mathbf{K}$ is not zero we may take the phenomenon of sedimentation equilibrium under gravity. A suspension of Brownian particles in a vessel if left undisturbed will, whatever the initial distribution, gradually approach an equilibrium in which the concentration of particles decreases exponentially with height. If we take the z-direction as the upward vertical the external force is $\mathbf{K} = -m'g$, where m' is the effective mass of a Brownian particle, allowing for buoyancy. In its essentials the problem is a one-dimensional one and the Smoluchowski equation becomes

$$\frac{\partial n_1}{\partial t} = \frac{\partial}{\partial z}\left(\frac{kT}{\alpha}\frac{\partial n_1}{\partial z} + \frac{m'g}{\alpha}\,n_1\right) \qquad 10.8$$

When equilibrium is attained the left-hand side vanishes and in this case it is readily verified that the bracket on the right also vanishes when $n_1 = \text{const}\,\exp\,(-m'gz/kT)$. This is the Halley formula, or law of isothermal atmospheres, which we have already encountered in ch. 2. The full solution of the time-dependent equation (10.8) for a particular initial distribution has been given by Chandrasekhar,[3] with interesting graphical illustrations showing how the distribution at various times gradually approaches the equilibrium. One may describe this approach as a diffusion process biased by the external force $\mathbf{K}$. Acting alone gravity would eventually cause the particles to fall to the bottom of the vessel, while diffusion alone would spread them uniformly throughout the vessel. The Halley distribution represents the compromise between these tendencies.

The Smoluchowski equation describes only the variation of the coordinate distribution function, n_1, with time. A still more general problem would include also the variation of the velocity (or momentum) distribution of the particles. This general problem may be formulated as follows. Given the initial distribution function, $f_1(0)$, for both coordinates and momenta of the particles at $t=0$ together with the necessary information about the external forces, what will be the distribution $f_1(t)$ at any subsequent time t? The solution of this problem has been obtained by further generalising Einstein's and Smoluchowski's method and leads to a partial differential equation for $f_1(t)$ which contains partial derivatives of the momenta, as well as the coordinates and the time. This rather cumbersome equation is called the Fokker–Planck equation (sometimes also the Kramers–Chandrasekhar equation) and, except in simple cases, is rather difficult to solve. Fortunately, its solution is of little practical interest for Brownian movement studies. The friction constant, $6\pi\eta a$, for a Brownian particle is so large that, however great the initial velocity at $t=0$, most of it is rapidly lost—so rapidly that the coordinates of the particle scarcely have time to change from their initial values.

The velocity-distribution function therefore reaches an equilibrium much more quickly than the coordinate distribution—within a small fraction of a second. This equilibrium is the Maxwell distribution and when this is substituted into the Fokker–Planck equation it is found that it is reduced to the Smoluchowski equation. Provided, therefore, we do not consider times too near $t = 0$, the velocity distribution can be taken as the known Maxwell distribution and the only distribution function of interest from then on is the coordinate distribution, determined by the appropriate solution of Smoluchowski's equation.

After this digression let us return to the theory of liquids and see to what extent we can take over the ideas of Brownian movement theory. The first point of difference is that in Brownian movement theory the particles are regarded as independent, that is, they do not exert forces on each other. This means that, as in ideal gases, all the information of interest is contained in the singlet distribution functions $f_1(t)$ and $n_1(t)$. In liquid theory, however, we recall that the distribution functions for molecular pairs are the important ones, and particularly the configurational distribution n_2. The necessary modification in the mathematical procedures have been worked out by Kirkwood and Eisenschitz.[7] Instead of regarding, as heretofore, a single representative molecule as a Brownian particle the interpretation is now applied to a representative pair. The pair is subject to a fluctuating force, $F_2(t)$, which arises from the motion of the remaining $(N-2)$ particles of the system. The Brownian motion of the pair is described by introducing two sets of coordinates, one of which locates the centre of gravity of the pair, and the other, of greater physical significance, the position of one particle relative to the other. The fundamental assumption 10.1 is recast in the form of a statement that after the lapse of a characteristic small time interval the auto-correlation function of F_2 will have decayed to zero. The integral of the auto-correlation function over a time greater than the characteristic interval (but less than the Poincaré cycle) leads to a new friction constant, γ, corresponding to the previous α. These procedures provide the necessary statistical foundation for the formulation of a Fokker–Planck equation for the pair. Finally, on the assumption that the friction constant γ is large enough, this can be reduced to a Smoluchowski equation. When application to the special case of viscous flow is envisaged these derivations are made for a fluid in motion by supposing that the bulk velocity of the fluid is represented by a vector **c** which depends on the coordinates. After a lengthy analysis the Smoluchowski equation, in the relative coordinates, is

$$\frac{\partial \rho\,(r,\,\theta,\,\phi,\,t)}{\partial t}$$

$$= \mathrm{div}\left\{\frac{kT}{\gamma}\,\mathrm{grad}\,\rho(r,\,\theta,\,\phi,\,t) - \frac{[-\,\mathrm{grad}\,\psi + \gamma\mathbf{c}]}{\gamma}\,\rho(r,\,\theta,\,\phi,\,t)\right\} \quad 10.9$$

In spite of these additional complications the general resemblance of this equation to 10.7 is very marked. The introduction of the pair concept leads to the replacement of the singlet distribution function $n_1(t)$ by the pair distribution which, in turn, can be written in terms of the (now time-dependent) radial distribution function $\rho(r,\,\theta,\,\phi,\,t)$. The introduction of relative (polar) coordinates r, θ, ϕ, locates the position of one molecule of the pair with respect to the other chosen as the origin, and the friction constant α has been replaced by γ. Instead of an external force, **K**, acting on a Brownian particle there appears the mean relative force of one molecule on the other, which is written as the negative gradient of the potential of average force, $-\,\mathrm{grad}\,\psi$ (p. 132). The term $\gamma\mathbf{c}$ is due to the superimposed bulk velocity of the fluid, which can be regarded as exerting a differential dragging effect on each of the molecules of the pair and so is added to the relative force term.

For thermodynamic equilibrium the left-hand side of 10.9 vanishes, as does the bulk velocity **c**. It is then readily verified that the expression in the curly bracket also vanishes if $\rho(r,\,\theta,\,\phi,\,t) = \rho(r) = \rho_0 \exp(-\psi/kT)$, the ordinary relation between the equilibrium distribution and potential of average force (p. 132, eq. 8.18) whose form is analogous to the Halley formula.

To apply the theory to viscosity we give the bulk velocity vector **c** the appropriate form for the steady laminar flow of fig. 9.1, that is, $c_x = G_{xy}\,.\,y$ with $c_y = c_z = 0$, where the velocity gradient can be chosen as small as we please, since the liquid is presumed to be Newtonian. As the flow is steady, that is, not time-dependent, the slightly-distorted radial distribution function is also independent of time and becomes $\rho(r,\,\theta,\,\phi)$, and the left-hand side of 10.9 again vanishes. (This steady non-equilibrium state must not be confused with the state of thermodynamic equilibrium.) The small perturbation of the equilibrium distribution can now be given the form of eq. 9.16 and inserted in the Smoluchowski equation. On expressing the vector operators in spherical polar coordinates the angular functions can be cancelled throughout, and the following ordinary differential equation is obtained for the radial part of the distortion, $u(r)$,

$$\frac{d^2u}{dr^2} + \left(\frac{2}{r} - \frac{1}{kT}\frac{d\psi}{dr}\right)\frac{du}{dr} - \frac{6u}{r^2} = \frac{\gamma}{(kT)^2} \cdot r \cdot \frac{d\psi}{dr} \qquad 10.10$$

This equation has been obtained by both Kirkwood and Eisenschitz[7] and its solution, when inserted in 9.18, should furnish a value for the viscosity if the numerical value of the friction constant is presumed known.

There are, however, formidable difficulties still to be overcome. In the first place, the differential equation for $u(r)$ is of the second order and therefore requires two boundary conditions in order to determine a unique solution. There is general agreement that one of these is that $u(r) \to 0$ as $r \to \infty$, the distortion must vanish at large distances. There is, however, disagreement about the second condition. Kirkwood, Buff and Green[8] assumed that $u(r) \to 0$ as $r \to 0$ while Eisenschitz[9] applies a second stronger condition at infinity, namely $r^3 u(r) \to 0$ as $r \to \infty$. This makes $u(r)$ infinite at the origin, but the calculated viscosity can still remain finite. We shall not go into the arguments used to support these alternative conditions and merely say that they lead to different functions for $u(r)$ and so affect the calculated viscosity, and that it appears probable that the strong condition is more likely to be correct. Secondly, in spite of many attempts to calculate it, the friction constant, γ, is at present uncertain to within an order of magnitude or so and little is known about its temperature dependence, though it is probable that this is not very strong. Finally, the Smoluchowski equation and the viscosity integral (9.18) contain the imperfectly-known radial distribution function for equilibrium $\rho(r)$, or the related quantity $\psi(r)$.

The experimental value of the shear viscosity of liquid argon at $89°K$, near the normal boiling point, is $2 \cdot 39 \times 10^{-3}$ poise. In a first calculation, by Kirkwood, Buff and Green[8] a value of the friction constant for argon of $4 \cdot 84 \times 10^{-10}$ gm sec^{-1} was estimated, by making certain assumptions about the fluctuating force. This gave a viscosity of $1 \cdot 27 \times 10^{-3}$ poise, about one-half the experimental value. These authors also calculated the contribution of the kinetic part of the momentum flow and found that it amounted to only about 2% of the calculated viscosity. A later calculation by Zwanzig, Kirkwood, Stripp and Oppenheim[10] gave $\gamma = 2 \cdot 85 \times 10^{-10}$ gm sec^{-1}.

These authors adjusted their radial distribution function so as to give a better agreement with the pressure as calculated from 8.3 and used this adjusted function to determine the viscosity. They found $\eta = 0.73 \times 10^{-3}$ poise, about one-third of the experimental value. These calculations were made for a $u(r)$ determined by the weak boundary condition.

Eisenschitz and his co-workers have also made estimates of γ by various methods and have obtained values ranging from 3.7×10^{-12} gm sec^{-1} to 5.67×10^{-11} gm sec^{-1}. The calculation of the viscosity is somewhat uncertain because of the divergence of $u(r)$ near the origin which appears when the strong boundary condition is applied. Using a value of γ of 2.3×10^{-11} gm sec^{-1}, obtained by Eisenschitz and Wilford[11] from an application of the collective coordinate technique, an estimate of $\eta = 1.91 \times 10^{-3}$ poise has been made.

The divergence of $u(r)$ near the origin appears implausible on physical grounds and this is attributed to a failure of the Smoluchowski equation in this region. As indicated above, this equation is only a good approximation to the Fokker–Planck equation if the friction constant is large. For Brownian motion this causes no difficulty but the uncertainty in the value of γ in liquid theory makes the replacement of the Fokker–Planck equation by the Smoluchowski equation more dubious. At the time of writing work is in progress to surmount these and other obstacles.

We may finally again mention that we have considered only the Kirkwood–Eisenschitz theory in the specific context of liquid shear viscosity, but that applications have been made to other irreversible processes, such as thermal conductivity. Although numerical results are not yet of high accuracy the theory provides at present perhaps the most satisfactory picture of irreversible behaviour in liquids at the molecular level. It is still too early to say whether this theory will eventually provide accurate values of the transport coefficients of liquids or whether some alternative approach[12] will ultimately be more successful.

BIBLIOGRAPHY

GENERAL REFERENCES

1 *Molecular Theory of Gases and Liquids.* J. O. Hirschfelder, C. F. Curtiss and R. B. Bird. J. Wiley, New York; Chapman and Hall, London 1954
2 *Liquids and Liquid Mixtures.* J. S. Rowlinson. Butterworth, London 1959
3 *L'État Liquide de la Matière.* E. Darmois. Albin Michel, Paris 1943
4 *An Advanced Treatise on Physical Chemistry.* J. R. Partington. Longmans Green, London 1951
5 *Molecular Theory of Fluids.* H. S. Green. North-Holland, Amsterdam 1952
6 *Lattice Theories of the Liquid State.* J. A. Barker. Pergamon, London 1963
7 *An Introduction to the Statistical Theory of Fluids.* G. H. A. Cole. Pergamon, London 1965
8 *Heat and Thermodynamics.* M. W. Zemansky. McGraw-Hill 1957
9 *Statistical Mechanics.* J. E. Mayer and M. G. Mayer. J. Wiley (N.Y.); Chapman and Hall (Lond.) 1940
10 *Elementary Principles in Statistical Mechanics.* J. W. Gibbs (1902). Dover Books (reprint), New York 1960
11 *Principles of Statistical Mechanics.* R. C. Tolman. O.U.P. 1938
12 *Statistical Mechanics.* T. L. Hill. McGraw-Hill, New York 1956

CHAPTER 1

1 Newton's *Opticks*, Query 31
2 F. A. Holland, J. A. W. Huggill and G. O. Jones, *Proc. R. Soc.* (A), **207**, 268, 1951.   J. S. Dugdale and F. E. Simon, *Proc. R. Soc.* (A), **218**, 291, 1953. D. W. Robinson, *Proc. R. Soc.* (A), **225**, 393, 1954

CHAPTER 2

1 General reference 4, Vol. I, p. 660
2 Gen. ref. 1, p. 131
3 See e.g. W. Magie, *A Source Book in Physics*. McGraw-Hill, New York 1935
4 C. A. Winkler and O. Maass, *Can. J. Res. 9*, 613, 1933. Gen. ref. 1, p. 374
5 Gen. ref. 1, p. 895
6 Gen. ref. 1, p. 357. Gen. ref. 4, Vol. I, p. 677
7 Gen. ref. 9, chs. 7 and 8

CHAPTER 3

1 F. Zernicke and J. A. Prins, *Z. Phys.* **41**, 184, 1927. Gen. ref. 1, p. 898
2 A. Eisenstein and N. S. Gingrich, *Phys. Rev.* **58**, 307, 1940; **62**, 261, 1942
3 K. Furakawa, *Rep. Prog. Phys.* **XXV**, 395, 1962
4 G. O. Jones, *Glass*. Methuen, London 1956
5 R. O. Davies and G. O. Jones, *Advances in Physics*, **2**, 370, 1953
6 F. E. Simon and F. Lange, *Z. Phys.* **38**, 227, 1926
7 A. G. Oblad and R. F. Newton, *J. Amer. Chem. Soc.* **59**, 2495, 1937

CHAPTER 4

1 F. O. Rice and E. Teller, *The Structure of Matter*. J. Wiley, New York; Chapman and Hall, London 1949
2 F. London, *Z. Phys. Chem.* (B), **11**, 222, 1930. *Trans. Far. Soc.* **33**, 8, 1937. Gen. ref. 1, p. 955
3 Gen. ref. 1, p. 1110. E. R. Dobbs and G. O. Jones, *Rep. Prog. Phys.* **XX**, 516, 1957

CHAPTER 5

1 Gen. refs. 8–12
2 Gen. ref. 10, p. 187. J. de Boer, *Rep. Prog. Phys.* **XII**, 305 (1948–9)
3 Gen. ref. 9, ch. 10

CHAPTER 6

1 Gen. ref. 9, chs. 13, 14. Gen. ref. 1, ch. 3
2 Gen. ref. 6
3 H. Eyring and J. O. Hirschfelder, *J. Phys. Chem.* 41, 249, 1937. Gen. ref. 1, p. 279
4 J. E. Lennard–Jones and A. F. Devonshire, *Proc. R. Soc.* (A), 163, 53, 1937; 165, 1, 1938. Gen. ref. 6, ch. 4
5 R. H. Wentorf, R. J. Buehler, J. O. Hirschfelder and C. F. Curtiss, *J. Chem. Phys.* 18, 1484, 1950. Gen. ref. 6, ch. 4
6 Gen. ref. 6
7 Gen. ref. 6. J. M. H. Levelt and E. G. D. Cohen in *Studies in Statistical Mechanics.* Ed. J. de Boer and G. E. Uhlenbeck. North Holland, Amsterdam 1964. Vol. 2, p. 111

CHAPTER 7

1 N. Metropolis, A. W. Rosenbluth, M. N. Rosenbluth and A. H. Teller, *J. Chem. Phys.* 21, 1087, 1953. M. N. Rosenbluth and A. W. Rosenbluth, *J. Chem. Phys.* 22, 881, 1954
2 B. J. Alder and T. W. Wainwright, *J. Chem. Phys.* 27, 1208, 1957; 31, 459, 1959. See also W. W. Wood and J. D. Jacobson, *ibid.* 27, 1207, 1957
3 B. J. Alder and T. W. Wainwright in *Proc. Int. Symposium on Transport Processes in Statistical Mechanics.* Ed. I. Prigogine. Interscience, New York 1958, p. 97
4 For photographs of the 'molecular' motions see B. J. Alder and T. W. Wainwright, 'Molecular Motions,' *Sci. Amer.* Oct. 1959 (*Sci. Amer.* reprint No. 265)
5 W. W. Wood and F. R. Parker, *J. Chem. Phys.* 27, 720, 1957

CHAPTER 8

1 J. de Boer, *Rep. Prog. Phys.* XII, 305, 1948–9
2 J. Yvon, *Actualités scientifiques et industrielles.* Hermann et Cie, Paris 1935. M. Born and H. S. Green, *Proc. R. Soc.* (A), 188, 10, 1946
3 J. G. Kirkwood, *J. Chem. Phys.* 3, 300, 1935. G. H. A. Cole, *Rep. Prog. Phys.* XIX, 1, 1956
4 J. G. Kirkwood and M. B. Boggs, *J. Chem. Phys.* 10, 394, 1935
5 J. G. Kirkwood, E. K. Maun and B. J. Alder, *J. Chem. Phys.* 18, 1040, 1950. J. G. Kirkwood, V. A. Lewinson and B. J. Alder, *J. Chem. Phys.* 20, 929, 1952. R. W. Zwanzig, J. G. Kirkwood, K. F. Stripp and I. Oppenheim, *J. Chem. Phys.* 21, 1268, 1953; 22, 1625, 1954

6   A. A. Broyles, *J. Chem. Phys.* **33**, 456, 1960; **34**, 359, 1068, 1961; **35**, 493, 1961. A. A. Broyles, S. U. Chung and H. L. Sahlin, *J. Chem. Phys.* **37**, 2462, 1962
7   G. H. A. Cole, *Rep. Prog. Phys.* **XIX**, 1, 1956
8   J. K. Percus and G. J. Yevick, *Phys. Rev.* **110**, 1, 1958
9   D. Pines and D. Bohm, *Phys. Rev.* **85**, 338, 1951
10   G. D. Scott, *Nature*, **188**, 908, 1960; **194**, 956, 1962
11   D. G. Henshaw, *Phys. Rev.* **105**, 976, 1957; **111**, 1470, 1958; **119**, 9, 1960
12   G. D. Scott, A. M. Charlesworth and M. K. Mak, *J. Chem. Phys.* **40**, 611, 1964
13   J. D. Bernal and J. Mason, *Nature*, **188**, 910, 1960. J. D. Bernal, J. Mason and K. R. Knight, *Nature*, **194**, 957, 1962
14   J. D. Bernal, *Proc. R. Soc.* (A), **280**, 299, 1964

CHAPTER 9

1   Gen. ref. 4. Vol. 2, p. 95
2   N. F. Zhdanova. *Zh. éksper. teor. Fiz.* **31**, 724, 1956. R. Scott. Ph.D. Thesis, London 1959
3   *Mathematical Theory of Non-Uniform Gases.* S. Chapman and T. G. Cowling, Cambridge 1952
4   Gen. ref. 5, p. 139

CHAPTER 10

1   Newton's *Opticks*, Query 31
2   Gen. ref. 11, pp. 48, 102
3   S. Chandrasekhar, *Rev. Mod. Phys.* **15**, 1, 1943. Reprinted with other papers in *Selected Papers on Noise and Stochastic Processes.* Ed. N. Wax, Dover, New York 1954
4   J. G. Kirkwood, *J. Chem. Phys.* **14**, 180, 1946
5   Einstein's papers are collected in *Investigations on the Theory of the Brownian Movement.* A. Einstein. Dover, New York 1956
6   See ref. 3 above
7   See e.g. R. Eisenschitz, *Statistical Theory of Irreversible Processes.* O.U.P. 1958
8   J. G. Kirkwood, F. P. Buff and M. S. Green, *J. Chem. Phys.* **17**, 988, 1949
9   R. Eisenschitz and A. Suddaby, *Proc. 2nd Int. Congr. Rheol.* Butterworth, London 1954. Ref. 7 above
10   R. W. Zwanzig, J. G. Kirkwood, F. Stripp and I. Oppenheim, *J. Chem. Phys.* **21**, 2050, 1953
11   R. Eisenschitz and M. J. Wilford, *Proc. Phys. Soc.* **80**, 1078, 1962
12   For a review, see S. G. Brush, *Chem. Rev.* **62**, 513, 1962

INDEX